W9-DEA-402

BUILDING SUPPORT NETWORKS FOR THE ELDERLY

SAGE HUMAN SERVICES GUIDES, VOLUME 36

SAGE HUMAN SERVICES GUIDES

a series of books edited by ARMAND LAUFFER and CHARLES GARVIN. Published in cooperation with the University of Michigan School of Social Work and other organizations.

A **SAGE** HUMAN SERVICES GUIDE **36**

WARNER MEMORIAL LIBRARY
EASTERN COLLEGE
ST. DAVIDS. PA. 19087

BUILDING SUPPORT NETWORKS FOR THE ELDERLY

Theory and Applications

David E. BIEGEL
Barbara K. SHORE
Elizabeth GORDON

Foreword by Gorham L. Black, Jr.

Published in cooperation with the University of Michigan School of Social Work

SAGE PUBLICATIONS
Beverly Hills   London   New Delhi

5-13-86

Copyright © 1984 by Sage Publications, Inc.

All rights reserved. No part of this book may be reproduced or utilized in any form or by any means, electronic or mechanical, including photocopying, recording, or by any information storage and retrieval system, without permission in writing from the publisher.

For information address:

SAGE Publications, Inc.
275 South Beverly Drive
Beverly Hills, California 90212

SAGE Publications India Pvt. Ltd.
C-236 Defence Colony
New Delhi 110 024, India

SAGE Publications Ltd
28 Banner Street
London EC1Y 8QE, England

Printed in the United States of America

Library of Congress Cataloging in Publication Data

Biegel, David E.
    Building support networks for the elderly.

    (Sage human services guides ; v. 36)
    "Published in cooperation with the University of
Michigan School of Social Work."
    Bibliography: p.
    1. Aged—Services for—United States. 2. Aged—United
States—Care and hygiene. 3. Social work with the aged—
United States. 4. Volunteer workers in social service—
United States. I. Shore, Barbara K. II. Gordon,
Elizabeth. III. Title. IV. Series.
HV461.B54   1984   362.6   84-8337

ISBN 0-8039-2350-3 (pbk.)

FIRST PRINTING

HV 1461 .B54 1984
Biegel, David E.
Building support networks
 for the elderly

CONTENTS

FOREWORD

Long before substantial resources became available to provide formal social services in our country, it was often families, friends, and neighbors who shouldered the burden of supplying support to needy persons in the community. Today, social workers commonly point to these same groups as good examples of what have come to be called "community support systems" or "social networks."

Human service practitioners have only recently come to understand fully the potential community support systems offer for helping to meet the needs of our elderly population. Developing and strengthening these social networks therefore becomes a logical step toward improving the quality of life of older persons in need.

The Pennsylvania Department of Aging became interested in the concept of building and using informal support systems because these systems can reduce community dependence on government-funded services and, at the same time, provide quality care to those who need it most. As part of its interest in this concept, the department contracted with the University of Pittsburgh's School of Social Work to develop a manual service practitioners could use as a resource to sharpen their ability to use social networks. I am pleased to see that much of the information contained in this book is the result of that cooperative effort. More important, I am confident that the material presented here will be used to serve older persons better.

—Gorham L. Black, Jr.
Secretary, Pennsylvania Department of Aging

ACKNOWLEDGMENTS

This volume grew out of a contract between the Commonwealth of Pennsylvania, Department of Aging and the University of Pittsburgh School of Social Work. Our work involved the development of training programs and resource materials for service providers on the use of informal support systems with the frail elderly. We are very appreciative of the assistance we received from the Department of Aging and of the leadership the department has provided in stimulating the use of informal support systems in service delivery with the elderly. In implementing this project, we requested program information from a number of projects around the country. We received an enormous amount of materials about many projects that utilize informal support systems in work with the elderly. The agencies that assisted us are too numerous to acknowledge individually. This volume would not have been possible, however, without the materials they provided. We are also grateful to Dean David E. Epperson for his support and encouragement. Charles Garvin, Acting Editor of the Sage Human Services Guides series, provided valuable feedback and suggestions that aided us in our work. Finally, we acknowledge the substantial assistance of Mary Pat Campbell, who typed numerous drafts of the manuscript.

INTRODUCTION

Over the past decade an increasing amount of research has been conducted in a variety of disciplines focusing on the role played by informal supports in moderating the deleterious effects of stress on health and mental health status. We now have a better understanding of the role and function of informal support systems and the ways in which human service practitioners can help to stimulate and strengthen them.

In the field of aging particularly there is much interest in developing mechanisms through which workers in the aging network can increase their knowledge of informal support systems and also enhance their skills in working with these systems. Therefore, in fiscal 1983 the Commonwealth of Pennsylvania, Department of Aging, as part of its continued interest in developing and strengthening informal supports for the elderly, contracted with the University of Pittsburgh School of Social Work to develop resource materials and implement a training program on the use of informal support systems with the frail elderly for the staff of Area Agencies on Aging throughout the state.

Three two-day training workshops were held and attended by 75 service providers from 41 agencies across the state. The training was very well received, and practitioners seemed eager for specific information about interventive strategies, examples of how these strategies work in practice, and suggestions of issues to consider in making use of these interventive methods. A number of Pennsylvania agencies were already utilizing some of these techniques, and their sharing of pertinent information was enthusiastically received by interested staff from other agencies.

Based on our experiences in conducting this training and in developing resource materials for practitioners, it became apparent that human service workers both within and without the aging network could benefit from a practitioners-oriented volume on social network intervention with the elderly. We hope that this volume will serve as a valuable resource for agency service providers by stimulating an appreciation for the need to develop and strengthen informal supports for the elderly and by inspiring the development of innovative informal support strategies. We include numerous examples of innovative and successful aging projects operated by a variety of service providers, and practical guidelines and suggestions for workers and agencies interested in implementing these interventions.

The work builds on knowledge and experience derived from many sources. As part of our research, an exhaustive effort was made to collect information on existing programs and models that address the social support needs of the elderly. The volume reflects the richness of these materials and draws on intervention models currently being applied throughout the United States, many of which should be noted for their creativity and ingenuity in meeting the needs of the elderly in a variety of settings.

A typology of social network interventions with the elderly was developed to help organize and systematize this abundance of material and make it useful for agency practitioners. The typology builds on the work of one of the coauthors and is meant to provide a framework to guide agency personnel so that they can create appropriate network interventions in their professional practice.

This volume consists of ten chapters. Chapter 1 provides background information about the growth of interest in social networks; definitions, roles, and functions of social networks and support systems; and a review of existing knowledge about social support and the elderly. As such, this chapter introduces the reader to the basic concepts necessary for a fuller understanding of what social networks are, why they are important, and how they function in relation to the elderly. Chapter 2 provides materials and tools for workers to use in assessing the strengths and weaknesses of the networks of both individuals and communities, and presents a discussion of evaluative strategies to measure the effectiveness of intervention programs.

The rest of the volume focuses on social network interventions. Chapter 3 presents a typology of social network interventions with the elderly, followed by a discussion of professional roles and implementation issues in using these interventive modalities. Six figures (Figures 3-8) are included and serve as reference material for succeeding chapters. Chapters 4 through 10 focus on the specific intervention modalities identified in the typology. Each chapter includes an overview of the intervention modality, followed by a number of examples of projects that utilize this intervention. Two sections then follow that are aimed at assisting practitioners to implement these strategies. The first section discusses professional roles and the implications of these roles for practitioners; the second section discusses specific implementation issues—administrative support, evaluative indicators, obstacles and limitations, and cautions.

Chapter 1

SOCIAL NETWORKS: AN OVERVIEW

In order to provide a framework for understanding how social networks function in relation to the elderly, the first part of this chapter provides background on the growth of interest in social networks; the definitions, roles and functions of social networks; and overall practice knowledge specific to social networks and the elderly.

The 1960s witnessed a tremendous growth in the number and variety of human service programs. New initiatives were developed in health, mental health, welfare, education, community development, and other areas. Despite this growth, we learned during the 1970s that human needs are larger and more extensive than can be met by the resources of agencies and professionals alone.

In the 1970s we also learned that the tremendous growth of needed services, many of these targeted at particular age groups or at individuals with special problems, while meeting many needs, brought with it some negative by-products. This proliferation led to problems of accessibility, fragmentation of services, and lack of accountability. At the same time we were discovering the inadequacy of the human services system and of some of the reform efforts, we were also rediscovering the important role of informal service providers—family, friends, neighbors, natural helpers, self-help groups, ethnic and fraternal organizations, neighborhood organizations and

AUTHORS' NOTE: This chapter is based upon previously published works of David Biegel. For further information, see: Biegel (in press) Biegel & Naparstek (1982) and Maguire & Biegel (1982).

the like. The last decade has witnessed an explosion of research and demonstration efforts focused on the role of these informal caregivers or "social networks."

As we move into the 1980s, human services are under attack and human service budgets are being cut. At the same time, economic pressures on individuals and families are taking their toll. When unemployment goes up, so do mental health problems, incidences of spouse and child abuse, and rates of suicide. Social networks cannot make up for cuts in needed public and private resources and will not be effective if they are used in this way, but they can help us to improve service delivery to those in need and to address the issues of fragmentation, lack of accessibility, and lack of accountability.

THE GROWTH OF INTEREST IN SOCIAL NETWORKS

In recent years there has been increasing interest and a concomitant "explosion" of conference papers, journal articles, books, and research projects concerned with the role of social networks in social welfare. The first major works about networks were by British anthropologists J. A. Barnes and Elizabeth Bott in the 1950s (Barnes, 1954; Bott, 1957). It was not until the late 1960s, however, that the network concept attracted significant attention. A 1978 bibliography on networks contains over 1,500 entries, of which few were dated before 1965. There is now a journal devoted to this field—*Social Networks*—and a new professional organization—the INSNA, or International Network for Social Network Analysis (Wolfe, 1978).

Often the more things change, the more they stay the same. Social networks are not a new phenomenon. The first mutual aid group, the Scots Charitable Society, was formed in 1657. Strengthening neighborhood support systems was a major goal of the Settlement House Movement led by social workers in the early twentieth century. What is new in the 1980s, however, is renewed interest and involvement with such support systems, coupled with an expanded knowledge base in this area. This has occurred for a number of reasons.

First, there is a growing awareness that human service needs cannot be met by professionals alone. For example, in the mental health area in any given year at least 15% of the population shows symptoms of mental illness (President's Commission on Mental Health, 1978). If mild or moderate anxieties and upsets are included, the rates become much higher. Yet if all available professional mental health resources were deployed maximally, no more than 3% of the population could receive professional care at any given time. It is clear that alternative strategies, such as the utilization of informal helping networks, must be developed to counter our overreliance on clinical treatment by professionals if those in need are to be served adequately.

Second, there is increasing societal interest in individuals assuming more responsibility for the maintenance of their own health. The U.S. Surgeon General's Annual Report in 1979, on the status of health in the U.S. population, placed heavy emphasis on prevention of illness and promotion of positive health. "Doing it yourself," an outgrowth of the human potential movement of the 1970s, is in vogue, and self care as well as self-help activities are growing.

Third, America, the land of "good and plenty," has had to realize— painful as that may be—that its resources, fiscal and human, are not unlimited. We have begun to acknowledge that dollars alone cannot provide for meeting all human needs and that government agencies and programs are limited in their ability to solve pressing social problems. This has led to a sense of frustration, as well as to a willingness to explore alternative approaches to meeting human needs.

We are now beyond the point of arguing whether agency professionals should work with informal service providers in the community. This has now been accepted as proper and appropriate by service providers. Informal networks already provide a far greater amount of help to those in need than do professional services. In the last several years, an increasing number of human service providers have become involved in strengthening and/or creating informal support systems in the community. For such efforts to succeed, there must be development and sustenance of partnerships between informal and professional support systems. Strategies for the creation of such partnerships are discussed extensively in this volume.

SOCIAL NETWORKS AND SUPPORT SYSTEMS— DEFINITIONS, ROLES, AND FUNCTIONS

There is not any single, uniformly agreed-upon definition of social network. Barnes (1972) and Mitchell (1969) define social network from a structural perspective. Barnes says a network is "a set of points which are joined by lines; the points of the image are people or sometimes groups and the lines indicate which people interact with each other" (Barnes, 1972, p. 43). Thus the units within networks need not be individuals. Bott's (1957) research examined married couples; Craven and Wellman (1973) looked at the city as the unit of study. Mitchell defines social networks slightly differently than does Barnes, emphasizing their utility in understanding behavior. He states that a social network is a "specific set of linkages among a defined set of persons with the additional property that the characteristics of these linkages may be used to interpret the social behavior of the persons involved" (Mitchell, 1969, p. 2). Walker (1977) defines social network in terms of both content and outcome of interactions. He states that an individual's social network is "that set of personal contacts through which the individual maintains his social identity and receives emotional support, material aid and services, information and new social contacts" (p. 35).

Thus a social network consists of people in interaction and may be defined neutrally in terms of structure or in terms of outcome. Walker's perspective seems to fit with existing applications of networks in social welfare and will be used as the frame of reference here. We use the term "social networks" almost synonymously with community support systems—family, friends, neighbors, coworkers, natural helpers, community gatekeepers, self-help groups, clergy and religious institutions.

An important influence on the growing literature dealing with community support systems and social support has been the seminal theoretical contributions of Gerald Caplan (1974, 1976). Caplan describes support systems as health-promoting forces at the person-to-person and social levels that enable people to master the challenge and strains of their lives. Caplan's research on how individuals respond to crises in their lives led him to the conclusion that response to a crisis by an individual is dependent on three factors: (1) the nature and vicissitudes of stress, (2) the current ego strength of the individual, and (3) the quality of emotional support and task-oriented assistance provided by the individual's social network. Of these three factors, Caplan found the last—the role of the social network—to be most significant. In examining how support systems operate Caplan states that social support (the product of a support system) can be ongoing and continuous or intermittent and short term. Both enduring and short-term supports, according to Caplan, consist of three elements:

— The significant others help the individual mobilize his psychological resources and master his emotional burdens.

— They share his tasks.

— They provide him with extra supplies of money, materials, tools and skills, and cognitive guidance to improve his handling of the situation (Caplan, 1974, pp. 5-6).

We must keep in mind, however, that not all ties are supportive, and only a minority of ties are significantly supportive (Wellman, 1981). Nevertheless, interaction with trusted others is essential to individual well-being throughout one's life. Each of us needs others for survival. These significant others may be family, friends, relatives, neighbors, or coworkers on whom one consistently and differentially relies.

Relationships with others serve a variety of functions for individuals. Among those cited by the President's Commission on Mental Health (1978) as particularly noteworthy are "meaningful attachment to significant others; social integration in a network of common interest relationships; an opportunity for the nurturance of others, especially children; reassurance of individual worth gained through the performance of a social role; a sense of reliable alliance with kin; access to the obtaining of guidance from trustworthy and authoritative persons in times of stress."

Examples of community support systems elements are as follows:

— The woman in her 60s on the block to whom parents turn for advice in raising their children.

— The bartender to whom customers talk about their marital problems.

— The self-help group for parents who have adopted children with special needs that allows members to share experiences, frustrations, successes, and failures.

— The widowed persons group the church sponsors to provide mutual support and socialization.

— The neighbor who helps an older person with shopping and household tasks.

— The natural helper who assists neighbors to apply for and receive social security benefits.

— The clergyman to whom parishioners talk about the burdens of caring for an aged parent.

— The community organization that helps residents develop a needed community-based hotline.

— The ethnic organization that helps middle-aged parents with the strains caused by value conflicts with their children.

In a pluralistic society, people seek help, solve problems, and meet needs in different ways. Family; friends; neighbors; mutual helpers; community gatekeepers; coworkers; clergy and religious institutions; neighborhood, ethnic, fraternal, or social organizations; and, mutual aid groups can all provide meaningful assistance in times of need and are encompassed in the term "community support systems." Community support systems can serve preventive, treatment, and rehabilitative functions. On a *preventive* level, they can contribute to an individual's sense of well-being and competent functioning. They can assist in reducing the negative consequences of stressful life events. Thus the mother who is experiencing the burdens of raising her own family while also providing care for her aged father can be aided through an educational and training program aimed at parents in similar situations. On a *treatment* level, community support systems can play an adjunctive role to professional care through positive reinforcement and assistance to individuals in following treatment plans. Thus family members and friends can assist the agency worker to help aged individuals to take their medication properly as prescribed by their doctors. On a *rehabilitative* level, community support systems can help reintegrate individuals with chronic mental health problems back into the community. This is an especially critical issue for older persons released from mental hospitals after stays of 20 or 30 years or longer.

Community support systems operate on both one-to-one and group levels. On the one-to-one level, community support systems are often "natural" caregiving efforts that are ongoing and develop and function without support or assistance from human service professionals. Such supportive relationships may exist between a friend and neighbor, grandfather and grandson, pastor and parishioner, teacher and parent, neighborhood leader and group member, and between coworkers, to name but a few. Sometimes informal support systems on the one-to-one level are established through the intervention of a human service professional who assists an individual in need, who is isolated from a supportive network in the community, to develop ties with clergy, neighbors, or natural helpers. Once formed, these ties often continue without the need for ongoing professional intervention.

Group forms of community support systems, such as groups for families of patients with Alzheimer's disease, widowed or divorced persons, alcoholics, or former mental patients, are sometimes organized and developed with the assistance of human service professionals. Many times, however, they develop without professional invervention. These groups help the individuals in need to realize that they are not alone, that others share their problems and needs, and that others often have experience dealing successfully with the same issues with which they are struggling.

Participation in these groups varies by the needs and interests of group members. Some individuals stay in the group for a short period until they can cope on their own with another situation; others remain for ongoing friendship and social activities. The type of participation also varies by group. In some groups, members are expected to remain for long periods (or a lifetime)—for example, Alcoholics Anonymous. Alcoholics, the AA philosophy states, can never be cured and thus need an ongoing support group. Other groups like Parents Without Partners, a support group for single parents, fully expect a rapid turnover in membership as many members either remarry or are able to function independently with the help of the group and the informal relationships and friendships made through the group.

Although individuals receive assistance through formal group activities and programs, much of the support in these groups is informal as particular individuals develop friendships, social relationships, and enhance their support systems. One extremely significant advantage of self-help groups is that many of the individuals who join these groups and receive help might never go to professionals for assistance, for a variety of reasons. Other groups exist that may not be organized for self-help purposes, but participation in these groups becomes an important element of an individual's support system and provides much help and sustenance. Ethnic clubs, PTAs, neighborhood organizations, and social and fraternal groups can all provide important elements of support. There is evidence that individuals who are members of organizations experience fewer symptoms of mental illness than do individuals who are not group members.

Community support systems are found everywhere. They exist in low-, middle-, and high-income communities and in rural, urban, and suburban areas. Community support systems cut across age, gender, ethnic, class and racial lines. Thus community support systems serve all of us to some degree in different ways. More specifically, however, community support systems serve many population groups that are unwilling or unable to seek professional help or for whom professional services currently may be lacking. Community support systems offer help in a culturally acceptable manner without stigma or loss of pride. The individuals seeking help do not need to identify themselves as having a problem, being weak, sick, a client, or a patient as when seeking professional help.

A brief overview of the research findings on social networks (Wellman, 1981; Granovetter, 1973) shows the following:

— People solve problems and meet needs in different ways—networks vary by age, gender, class, and ethnic grouping.

— Not all ties are supportive, and only a minority of ties are significantly supportive.

— People do not belong to just one network; individuals tend to belong to both densely knit clusters and more sparsely knit webs. Different types of ties—work, neighborhood, and kinship—tend to be separate from each other.

— Many ties are not chosen voluntarily but are embedded structurally in work situations, the neighborhood, kinship systems, and friendship circles; they may provide important resources but not necessarily affection.

— Most ties are asymmetric in content and intensity; there is rarely a one-to-one correspondence in exchange.

— Not all ties are *equivalently* supportive: Some ties are based on affection; while others are based on instrumental resources.

— Networks of "well" individuals are larger and stronger than are networks of the mentally ill.

— Networks are not static: There is a high rate of change in network membership, even in networks of greatest intimacy.

— We depend on specific individuals for different things; the more varied one's networks, the more one's privacy and secrecy are enhanced.

— Large, loose-knit networks appear to expedite access to tangible resources, whereas dense networks with strong ties expedite access to less tangible, emotional resources.

— Sometimes weak ties are more effective than strong ties for specific purposes; for example, for finding a job, weak ties may provide a wider range of resources and information.

SUPPORT SYSTEMS AND THE ELDERLY— EXISTING KNOWLEDGE

There is a large data base of knowledge concerning the role of support systems and the elderly. Here we will highlight particular findings especially relevant to an understanding of social network interventions. Special attention will be paid to "at-risk" subgroups of the elderly. Because professional resources are limited, decisions must always be made about how to target interventions for those most in need or at risk. Social network implications of recent demographic trends of the elderly will also be presented.

DEMOGRAPHIC TRENDS AND AT-RISK GROUPS

It is erroneous to think of the elderly as one homogeneous group. A number of researchers have pointed out the tremendous diversity within the elderly population (Kahn & Antonucci, 1981; Cantor, 1979; Palmore, 1974). In fact, older adults may be a more diverse group than other population groups. Variables identified by researchers as particularly relevant in differentiating subgroups of the elderly include gender, age (young-old, middle-old, and old-old), ethnicity, race, socioeconomic status, marital status, living status (alone versus with someone), and geographical location (urban versus rural).

The number and proportion of older (65 years and over) persons in the U.S. population has been increasing steadily since 1900. An increasing proportion of the aged are 75 years and older. In fact, population 75 years and older has been increasing at a rate even faster than that of the population 65-74 years, and the population 85 years and older has grown even faster. This faster rate of increase is expected to continue through the century. By the year 2000, the population 75-84 group will increase by 57%, and the 85 and older group will double in size (Brody, 1982). This trend is significant in terms of support systems because those 75 years and older are more likely to have health problems, require assistance in meeting the needs of daily living, live alone, and be at greater risk for institutionalization. At the same time, this group with the most need for assistance is least likely to have an adequate social network and is often underserved by professional services.

Women, as a subgroup of the elderly, are also at high risk. In fact, the old-old population contains far more women than men, and the women are more likely to be widowed or divorced, live alone, be poor, and be chronically ill (Nowak, 1983). Another subgroup of the elderly at high risk are minority elderly. They are said to suffer triple jeopardy—being old, poor, and in a minority. They are more likely to live in poverty and have more chronic health problems than are white elderly. Minority elderly also face more barriers to the utilization of professional services (Hooyman, 1983).

The elderly have greater need for social support than other population groups; yet overall, their social networks tend to be weaker than those of younger individuals. There are many stresses and losses affecting both mental and physical health in old age. In fact, one of the major issues for elderly that creates a need for intervention is the continuum of loss. In this continuum, over time aging persons begin to experience substantial losses in body functioning, sensory functioning, mental functioning, family and peer group supports, income, self-image, self-esteem, control, and power.

This continuum of loss begins to accelerate in the aging years, often to such a degree that an overload of loss is experienced. This overload of loss tends to have an interactional impact on elderly persons' functioning, as the overload itself often produces depression and grief that drains energy away from coping capacities. An additional factor that often operates for the older person is the loss of elasticity or ability to ''bounce back'' from losses (Shore, 1983). As a result, persons experience a diminution of their

Coping Skills

		Hi	Lo
Social Support	Hi	LR	MR
	Lo	MR	HR

FIGURE 1: Continuum of loss. KEY: HR = high risk; MR = medium risk; LR = low risk.

coping skills and capacities that may have served them well in earlier stages of life when more energy, elasticity, and functional capacities were present. In addition, it is a loss both of some of the coping skills that they possess—physical, emotional, psychological—and also of the social support network itself. Social functioning is a function of the interaction between available social supports and coping skills, as exhibited in Figure 1. In determining where the greatest need for intervention is, this figure helps to highlight the degree of vulnerability.

In facing the impact of the continuum of loss and the debilitating effects of the overload of losses that often are experienced by the elderly, it becomes clear that the substitution of social supports for coping skills can be an extremely important interventive plan (Shore & Raiff, 1977). Informal support systems, to a major degree in fact, can help individuals to cope with some of the losses that otherwise are overwhelming. The utilization of informal support systems to provide such support is therefore a key to the capacity to cope.

At the same time the elderly suffer these losses, they also make less use of professional services than do other population groups (Biegel, 1982; Antonucci & Bornstein, 1978; Kulka, 1978) and are likely to have weaker social supports than are nonelderly (Gore, 1978; Cassel, 1976; Dean & Lin, 1977; Eaton, 1978). This situation becomes compounded when one realizes that minorities, single persons, the poor, and those with little education are also at a disadvantage in terms of such support systems (Fischer, Jackson, Stueve, Gerson, Jones & Baldassare, 1977).

SUPPORT SYSTEM STRENGTHS

Despite the fact that the elderly generally have weaker systems of social support than do younger populations, most elderly persons do have some type of support system. Such systems are important in providing opportunities for socialization, assistance in carrying out the needs of daily living, and the provision of personal assistance during times of crisis (Cantor, 1979). As many researchers have shown, it is a myth that the elderly are abandoned by their families. Rather, family members provide extensive support and represent the elderly's most significant social resource (Brody, 1982; Shanas, 1979; Sussman, 1976; Cantor, 1979). Research shows that most basic and extended needs of the elderly are provided within the family network.

About one-third of the elderly live with a spouse. As one might expect, couples have the largest amount of interdependence, reciprocal caring, and general responsiveness to needs (Worts, 1982). Children of the elderly provide significant amounts of support, with children of frail elderly assuming an even larger portion of the care needs (Sussman, 1976). As Brody reports, the great majority of old persons live near at least one child and see their children frequently. These family members provide the great bulk (80%) of medically related personal care services for the noninstitutionalized elderly (Brody, 1982; U.S. General Accounting Office, 1977). In addition, as Brody states, ''not included in any calculation of services provided are emotional support, response in crisis, interest and concern and overall dependability—these are provided almost exclusively by families (1982, pp. 77-78).

Friends and neighbors are also significant providers of social support for the elderly (Baum & Baum, 1980; Biegel, 1982; Guttmann, 1982). In fact, because of their physical proximity, neighbors may be the most valuable resource to the elderly in times of emergency (Hooyman, 1983). The concept of neighborhood itself as a socialization center is very important to the elderly, especially ethnic elderly, many of whom have lived in the same neighborhood for long periods and who have been found to meet most of their social and daily needs within a six-block radius of their homes (Biegel, 1982; Cantor, 1972; Guttman, 1982; Lawton, 1973; Rosow, 1967).

Although the elderly participate in organizations to a lesser degree than do other population groups, community groups and associations nevertheless are important to the well-being of the elderly (Lopata, 1973; Lowenthal, 1968; Rose & Peterson, 1965; Shanas et al., 1968; Townsend, 1975). The church is of particular importance, with most participation in voluntary organizations by the elderly being church-related (Hendricks, 1977).

SUPPORT SYSTEM LIMITATIONS

There are a number of limitations and/or weaknesses in the informal support systems of the elderly. Specifically, these include the following: (1) A small but disturbing number of elderly are isolated and have no significant others to turn to for help and assistance. (2) Social and demographic trends may portend lessened availability of family support in the future. (3) Family members providing support may become overburdened by the strain of caring for an elderly relative. (4) Friends and neighbors may be unable to address long-term and specialized needs of the elderly. (5) Finally, existing informal support systems are often fragmented. Each of these concerns requires careful attention.

The isolated elderly. Research findings concerning informal support systems among the elderly have indicated that most elderly have at least one other individual—usually a family member, friend, or neighbor—to assist them when they have a problem or need. But what about individuals who do not have anyone to rely on? Guttmann (1982) studied help-seeking among eight white ethnic elderly groups and found that one-fifth (20%) of the sample had no one to turn to in a crisis. Cantor (1979) also found elderly individuals without a significant other or support system. However, only 8% of her sample fell into this category. Biegel (1982) found that significantly fewer elderly than younger individuals utilized informal helpers when facing a serious life crisis event. Although these elderly individuals are clearly a small minority, they are nonetheless at greater risk for health and mental health problems, as well as at greater risk for institutionalization.

The changing nature of the family. A number of demographic and social trends have been indicated by researchers as affecting the future availability of social support to the elderly from family members. These include increasing geographical distance between elderly and their children, smaller family sizes (i.e., fewer children to be caregivers for the elderly), increasing numbers of women in the workplace (women are the most frequent caregivers), higher divorce rates, and growth in the number of elderly who outlive their children (Gelfand & Gelfand, 1982; Slater, 1970; Smyer, 1982).

Family burden. There is a burgeoning amount of research relating to the issue of "family burden"—the strains felt by caregivers of the elderly (Brody, 1982; Butler, 1981; Gordon, 1981; Nowak, 1983; Smyer, 1982). The most significant problems for caregivers identified by researchers include coping with physical and mental illness and increased needs of the elderly, restrictions on social and leisure activities, disruption of household and work routines, conflicting multiple role demands (wife, mother, worker, and caregiver of parent or in-laws), lack of support and assistance from other family members, and lack of information and support from agency professionals on how to care for an aging parent.

Care by friends and neighbors. As the elderly grow older, so do their friends, who tend to be similar in age to themselves. Thus illness and death can weaken the friendship network when it is needed the most. Similarly, those elderly who live in age-segregated neighborhoods may have fewer young neighbors to assist them. Litwak (1979) notes that friends and neighbors may be unwilling and/or unable to make a long-term commitment of care to the elderly; nor are they able to provide assistance that requires equipment and/or expertise (i.e., skilled health care). Thus elderly individuals needing specialized care cannot realistically expect this care to be provided either by elderly friends or by neighbors.

Fragmentation of helping networks. In order for informal support systems in a community to be most effective, there should be linkages among family caregivers, neighbors, friends, clergy, and other helpers. Often this does not occur. Research on helping networks of the white ethnic elderly in Milwaukee (Biegel & Sherman, 1979) found that while there was much seeking and receiving of help by the elderly in the Southside Polish community, the helping networks were fragmented. Many helpers and leaders were unaware of the major problems of the elderly and of the helping networks they utilized for meeting their needs. For example, although many clergy provided support services to the elderly, individual clergy were not aware of other clergy only a block or two away who were providing similar supports to this same population group. In addition, clergy were almost totally unaware of "natural helpers" who were also providing supports for the elderly. Similarly, Guttmann (1979) found that ethnic leaders are often unaware of the needs and resources of the most at-risk elderly.

IMPLICATIONS OF PRACTICE KNOWLEDGE FOR NETWORK INTERVENTIONS

Interventions by professionals to strengthen support systems of the elderly should build on existing strengths, as well as address the limitations that have been identified above. Specifically:

— Professional interventions should be *geared to those elderly most at-risk*— those 75 years and over, especially women and black elderly, and those elderly without family, a confidante, or a significant other. In practice, however, this latter group is often difficult to locate and serve.

— Professional interventions should *recognize the significance of the continuum of loss* felt by the elderly and should develop interventions aimed at enhancing their coping capacity.

— Interventions should *strengthen the family's ability to provide support* to its elderly members and in so doing should attempt to relieve or reduce the stress of family burden. Such interventions will have to take into consideration the changing social and demographic characteristics of families and the expected new burdens of the future.

— Interventions should *strengthen the ability of friends, neighbors,* and other neighborhood-based caregivers to provide increased social support to the elderly, keeping in mind the realistic limitations of these providers. In this regard, new policy initiatives need to be developed, perhaps to reimburse community members willing to provide ongoing and skilled care to elderly members and to provide other needed supports to families.

— Professionals need to *strengthen existing networks* and enhance the coordination of informal and formal service providers to help overcome fragmentation of services.

In summary, the application of an informal support systems approach, both to strengthen informal supports and to create them when they do not exist, is a key method for avoiding undue debilitation and premature institutionalization of the elderly. It is a valuable tool to help deter movement from low risk to high risk. There is evidence that elderly persons are more likely to become institutionalized at the point at which the family burden becomes overwhelming, or at the point at which there is no family present, rather than at the point when their particular health status changes. Both the building of support systems to respond to the substantial need for support often experienced by older persons and the need to build assistance for the caregivers of the elderly are thus abundantly demonstrated in the literature and in practical experience. The response to the problems of older people cannot be to provide more and more formal supports: both money and program considerations make this unfeasible, if not undesirable.

EXERCISES AND STUDY QUESTIONS

1. The elderly are not one homogeneous population group. What subgroups of elderly do you see in your own or your agency's caseload?
2. For each subgroup of elderly:
    a. What are the most significant support system strengths (i.e., family, friends and neighbors, community groups, other)?

b. What are the most significant support system limitations (i.e., no significant others, family burden, lack of friends and neighbors, fragmentation of helping networks, other)?

c. Do these strengths and limitations differ among population subgroups? If yes, what are the major reasons?

SUGGESTED READINGS

Biegel, D., & Naparstek, A. (1982). *Community support systems and mental health: Practice, policy and research.* New York: Springer.

Brody, E. M. (1982). Older people, their families and social welfare. In *The social welfare forum, 1981.* New York: Columbia University Press.

Caplan, G. (1974). *Support systems and community mental health.* New York: Behavioral Publications.

Hooyman, N. (1983). Social support networks in services to the elderly. In J. K. Whittaker and J. Garbarino (Eds.), *Social support networks: Informal helping in the human services.* Hawthorne, NY: Aldine.

Wellman, B. (1981). Applying network analysis to the study of support. In B. Gottlieb (Ed.), *Social networks and social support.* Beverly Hills, CA: Sage.

Chapter 2

ASSESSMENT AND EVALUATION

Before one intervenes to reinforce and strengthen existing social networks or to create artificial networks for individuals with few or no significant others, an assessment of existing support systems must take place. This assessment can be viewed through two lenses. First, using an individually focused approach, an assessment can be conducted of the social network of an individual client of the agency. Second, using a community-level or public health approach, an agency can assess social networks of the elderly in a particular target area, focusing, perhaps, on a high-risk subpopulation group, such as elderly who are 75 years and older or those who are most isolated. The agency can then use this information to guide the development of programs and services.

These two approaches are complementary. Too often, however, practitioners use only one of these strategies. The first approach meets the needs of those elderly who have applied or been referred for service. The second approach helps uncover other elderly in the community who may need assistance but who have not been in contact with service agencies. It also helps to identify both informal and formal service providers who may be called on to help develop needed services. Each strategy will be discussed in turn.

THE INDIVIDUAL AS CLIENT

ASSESSMENT GOALS

In assessing an individual's social network, an agency should answer the following questions:

(1) What are the *strengths* of an individual's support system? The focus is on the kinds of resources being provided to the individual by his or her

network and the ways in which that network assists the individual in meeting the needs of daily living and in enhancing the quality of life.

(2) What are the *weaknesses* of an individual's support system? Here the concern is with the gaps and/or unmet needs that are not currently being provided for by the individual's network. The focus is on both the needs of daily living and the needs for love, affection, and companionship that are not being addressed fully by the network. These weaknesses may be due to lack of a sufficient number of individuals in the network, lack of sufficient involvement of network members, or lack of expertise of network members in tasks that involve specific technical skills (i.e., health care needs). Another important area to examine is the *potential* weaknesses of an individual's network. For example, is an elderly person depending primarily on a single individual in the network who may be old, in poor health, or moving to another community? Such a situation requires close monitoring by the service agency and perhaps the establishment of a special category of at-risk clients—namely, clients whose support systems are adequate at present but tenuous in terms of the future.

(3) What are the *obstacles* that prevent or inhibit the client from having a stronger support system? As the goal of the agency is strengthening of support systems, it is important to focus not only on strengths and weaknesses but also on factors that may act as stressors on the current support system. For example, perhaps the client's daughter is having difficulty assisting her father while working and raising her own family. She feels burdened and overwhelmed. This might suggest interventions by the agency to help the daughter support her father while also getting her own needs satisfied. (In Chapter 5 we discuss a variety of ways of enhancing the supports of the family caregiver.) In order to uncover obstacles to stronger networks, the agency needs to know not only that certain needs and wants are not being met but why, in the client's opinion, this is so. This information is critical to the development of intervention strategies. If possible, several key members of any client's network should also be interviewed in order to obtain an additional perspective on the obstacles issue.

ASSESSMENT TECHNIQUES

There are a number of ways in which the social networks of individuals can be assessed. In conducting assessments it is important for agencies to focus on both the *structure* and the *content* of an individual's social network. Structural variables include the number of ties, types of ties (kin, friends, neighbors, etc.), and the interconnectedness of ties, such as the

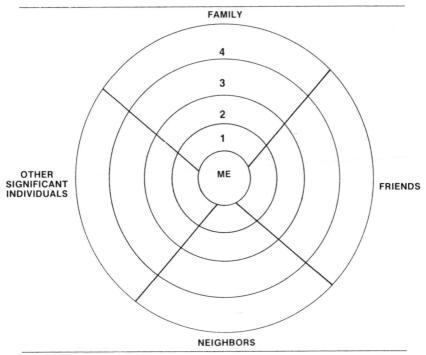

FIGURE 2: Social network map.

degree to which network members are connected to each other. Content variables focus on the kinds of assistance elderly persons receive from and give to their network for particular kinds of problems.

One technique that has been used for both research and practice purposes is the mapping of the client's social network. In our work, we have utilized a version of the mapping instrument developed by Todd (Curtis, 1979; see Figure 2). As can be seen, the diagram is divided into four sectors—family, friends, neighbors, and other significant persons (individuals such as mailman, beautician, bartender, and landlord who often play helpful roles in an individual's life). Each sector is further subdivided into four levels. The levels represent degrees of significance or importance of the relationship to the client. For each sector independently, level 1 represents the most significant ties and level 4 represents the least significant ties. Clients are asked to place the initials of all individuals with whom they have relationships in appropriate places on the map. They are then asked to draw lines connecting all individuals who have ties with each other.

Depending on the needs and abilities of the particular client, this map can be self-administered or completed by the client and worker together.

The resultant information provides data on the structure of the social network. To obtain information on the *content* of the client's social network, clients can then be asked to examine their map and indicate what kinds of assistance they receive for what kinds of problems, and also what kinds of help they give to others for what kinds of problems. Another way to obtain this information is to utilize the Activities of Daily Living (ADL) Schedule. Clients can be asked who provides assistance for each activity they cannot do by themselves and whether they are satisfied with the assistance they are receiving. Clients can also be asked about the nature of any problems or needs for which no one is available to help them, and why they cannot receive help for these problems.

Some agencies may prefer to conduct the assessment process using a standard intake form. In some states, each Area Agency on Aging develops and utilizes its own assessment form for intake purposes. As a result there is great variety in the amount and type of information collected about the individual's social network. In the state of Florida, all Area Agencies on Aging use a common assessment form. This form contains a section on services and social support, as follows:

(1) How much help per week are the clients receiving from their informal networks of family and friends?

(2) Who is primarily providing help?

(3) Is the client's informal network of family and friends able to continue giving this current level of help?

(4) Does the client's informal network of family and friends appear to be sufficiently resilient to respond to an increased demand for service in case of illness or accident?

These are important assessment questions. Additional questions that might be helpful to include are these: What kinds of help are being provided? By whom? For what specific tasks or needs? What tasks or needs are unmet? Why are these tasks or needs unmet? How satisfied is the client with his or her support system?

Biegel and Baum (1983), at the University of Pittsburgh School of Social Work, recently developed a lengthy research instrument that assesses both network structure and content. Although this instrument is too long for most service agencies to use as an assessment tool, it can be adapted for agency purposes. The following are some suggested questions that can be utilized in an assessment form:

---

(1) "Is there any one person you feel close to, who you trust and con- fide in, without whom it is hard to imagine life? Is there anyone else you feel very close to?"

(2) "Are there other people to whom you feel not quite that close but who are still important you?"

(3) For each individual named in 1 and 2 above, obtain the following:

    (a) Name

    (b) Gender

    (c) Age

    (d) Relationship

    (e) Geographic proximity

    (f) Length of time client knows individual

    (g) How do they keep in touch (in person, telephone, letters, combination)

    (h) Satisfaction with amount of contact—want more or less? "If not satisfied,
what prevents you from keeping in touch more often?"

    (i) "What does individual do for you?"

    (j) "Are you satisfied with the kind of support you get?"

    (k) "Are there other things that you think he or she can do for you?"

    (l) "What prevents him or her from doing that for you?"

    (m) "Are you also providing support to that individual? If so, what are you giving?"

(4) "Now, thinking about your network, all the people that you feel close to, would you want more people in it?

(5) "Are there any members of your network whom you would not want the Agency to contact? If so, who? Can you tell us why?

(6) "Are you a member of any groups or organizations? If so, which ones?"

(7) "Are you receiving assistance from any agencies? If so, what agen- cy and what service(s)?"

THE COMMUNITY AS CLIENT

ASSESSMENT GOALS

In assessing a community's social network, an agency should answer the following questions:

(1) What are the major problems or needs of at-risk population groups?

(2) What informal resources exist to meet those needs? What are the limitations of these informal supports?

(3) What formal resources exist to meet those needs? What are the limitations of these formal supports?

(4) What relationship exists between formal and informal resources?

(5) How can linkages be enhanced between informal and formal supports?

(6) What problems or needs are not currently being addressed by the formal and/or informal resources?

ASSESSMENT TECHNIQUES

A variety of techniques can be utilized for assessing social network resources, needs, and obstacles on a community-wide basis. These techniques are complementary and agencies should consider using a variety of strategies. Information collected should be geared toward the needs for which it is collected. Thus research instruments need to be adapted to program development and implementation purposes and vice versa. When thinking about these techniques, it is helpful to keep in mind the criteria the agency currently uses to determine community needs and develop programs. The key question then to ask is this: Will utilizing some of the strategies suggested below enhance the agency's ability to identify needs and develop programs?

Demographic analysis. The U.S. Census, conducted on a decennial basis, contains much valuable information that can help agencies identify at-risk population groups. Data can be analyzed by census tract or aggregated in larger units. Particular variables of interest include age, income, race, living status, housing stock, homeownership, percentage in poverty, and percentage recent movers. Comparisons of 1980 census data with 1970 and 1960 can be done for trend purposes. These data are available on a computerized basis that allows easy manipulation and reconfiguration of variables of interest. Resources that can assist agencies in preparing and utilizing these data include county planning agencies, community colleges and universities, and specialized research organizations. In every state, there are agencies that are designated as depositories of census tapes and materials that can be contacted for assistance.

Community surveys. Surveys can be conducted of a random sample of elderly in the community in order to assess their needs and resources. Such surveys can be expensive if they are not adapted to agency purposes. For example, a scientific survey of a random sample of community residents conducted by a survey research organization utilizing trained interviewers for a one-hour, in-person interview might cost from $50-$60 per respondent. Other, more inexpensive mechanisms can be utilized by agencies, however. The sample may not have to be drawn by random criteria, the questionnaire can be brief and designed for computer analysis, and the interviewers can be trained volunteers or students from a research class of a local college or university. The question is not whether the survey meets the criteria of the research method, but whether the information gathered adds to the agency's knowledge of informal support systems and unmet needs. It goes without saying that one must be extremely careful in interpreting interview results from a sample that is not randomly drawn. Agencies without in-house research and computer expertise might do well to consult with individuals having skills in this area. Colleges and universities can be asked to provide assistance to agencies in the development of the questionnaires and in analysis of the data.

The major advantage of this approach is that it provides data to the agency about at-risk groups of individuals who may not be asking the agency for assistance. It thus can help the agency identify needs and problem areas that should be addressed, such as the need to strengthen networks of the isolated elderly or to assist family caregivers of the frail elderly.

Client intake forms. If the agency gathers social network data on its intake form, then these forms can be aggregated to describe the networks of all of the agency's clients. This allows the agency to analyze any differences in network strengths, weaknesses, and obstacles across subpopulations of the elderly. For example what are the differences between male and female clients? Between those under 75 years and those older than 75 years? Between clients who live alone and those who don't? These analyses can help the agency identify unmet needs of at-risk population groups in its caseload.

Key informant survey. Another helpful assessment tool is to inverview individuals who, by virtue of their position in the community and/or service delivery system, are likely to have knowledge of the networks of aged individuals in the community. These key informants can be divided into three categories:

(1) *agencies*—staff from aging network agencies, as well as from health, mental health, and social service agencies.

(2) *gatekeepers*—clergy, pharmacists, physicians, and the like.

(3) *informal helpers*—natural helpers, neighborhood leaders, and so on.

This type of survey need not be costly. In fact, rather than surveying individuals on a one-to-one basis, groups of helpers can be gathered together for a needs assessment workshop in which, among other things, participants could complete self-administered questionnaires and work in groups to identify resources, needs, and obstacles. One advantage of a workshop, in addition to saving time and money, is that helpers can be mobilized to help plan and develop intervention strategies.

Typical survey questions might include the following:

---

(1) What are the three major problems of elderly in this community?

(2) For each problem:

    (a)   What do the elderly do who have this problem?

    (b)   What is the most helpful professional resource for addressing this problem?

    (c)   What is the most helpful informal resource?

    (d)   Are there sufficient resources for meeting this problem?

(3) What obstacles do elderly individuals in this community face that may prevent them from getting help when they need it?

(4) Are there any major problems of the elderly for which resources are not sufficient?

    (a)   If yes, what are these problems?

    (b)   What do you think can be done to address these problems?

Again, it must be stressed that the elderly are not a homogeneous population group. The above survey, therefore, may be altered to focus on particular subgroups of elderly. If this is not done, the above questions should be revised to collect data on the differences among the elderly population.

EVALUATION

Evaluation is an important and necessary component of all human services programs. Given that resources are always limited, any network intervention makes use of a fixed amount of scarce resources that cannot be used simultaneously for another purpose. In economics, this is referred to as "opportunity costs." It therefore behooves us to make sure that resources are being utilized wisely. Additionally, given that network interventions may represent a different way of conceptualizing practice, there is much we need to learn about the effectiveness of various intervention techniques to help improve service delivery. Finally, as human service professionals, we have an obligation to maximize the quality of services that we offer to clients. Evaluation is an ongoing tool for the improvement of practice. Evaluation planning should begin as soon as the assessment process is completed.

Suchman (1967) identified five criteria by which the success or failure of programs may be evaluated. These criteria are still very relevant and can be summarized as follows:

(1) *Effort* measures input or what was done. This is a necessary, though the simplest, type of evaluation. Examples of effort include number of hours of service offered, types of services offered, number and qualifications of staff, and number and types of clients served.

(2) *Performance* measures effect, or the results of the effort rather than the effort itself. This requires a clear statement of one's objective and a measure of change that occurred in relation to that objective. Performance is thus a measure of changes in clients as a result of services rendered.

(3) *Adequacy of performance* measures the degree to which performance is adequate to the total amount of need. This criterion is a ratio of the total number of individuals served by a particular service to the total number of individuals in the service area estimated as requiring the service.

(4) *Efficiency* is a measure of cost-effectiveness—could other intervention strategies be used that would obtain the same results but at a lower cost (i.e., money, time, personnel)?

(5) *Process* focuses on how and why a program works or does not work. Suchman states that this criterion is not an inherent part of evaluation research: nonetheless it can be very helpful in future program planning.

These criteria form a helpful reference function in planning. The effort criterion suggests the need for keeping adequate records so one can later analyze what was done. The performance criterion tells us that we must be clear about what we want to change and to make sure that our inputs (services) are adequate to bring about this change. The adequacy of performance criteria makes clear that our concern must not be only with clients who come to the agency for assistance, but also with the total needs in the community. When developing an intervention, the efficiency criterion makes clear the responsibility to explore other mechanisms or strategies to accomplish desired ends. Finally, the process criterion makes clear that we can learn from our failures as well as our successes and that it is important to measure both a program's successes and failures as well as to analyze why it does or does not work. In Chapters 4 through 10, evaluative criteria are suggested for each of the intervention strategies presented in this volume.

EXERCISES AND STUDY QUESTIONS

1. Complete a map of your own social network (see p. 29) and then answer the following questions: (a) What did you learn about your network? (b) How has your network changed in the past five years? What are the reasons for these changes? (c) How similar or different do you think your network map is from that of your own or your agency's elderly clients?

2. Thinking about networks on a community level, currently how does your agency assess the social networks of the elderly in your community? How could your agency utilize each of the following community assessment techniques: demographic analysis, community surveys, client intake forms and key informant survey? What advantages and disadvantages does each technique have for your agency? What are the obstacles in utilizing each of these techniques? How can these obstacles be overcome?

3. Which of the five evaluative criteria identified by Suchman (see p.35) does your agency utilize to evaluate its services? How can additional criteria be utilized? What obstacles do you see in utilizing these additional criteria? How can these obstacles be overcome?

SUGGESTED READINGS

Biegel, D., & Baum, M. (1983). *Social networks and the frail elderly interview schedule*. Pittsburgh: University of Pittsburgh, School of Social Work.
Suchman, E. A. (1967). *Evaluative Research*. New York: Russell Sage.

Chapter 3

A FRAMEWORK FOR STUDYING
NETWORK INTERVENTIONS

The remainder of this book focuses on intervention strategies to strengthen the social networks of the elderly. A conceptual framework that categorizes network interventions is provided in this chapter to help organize the myriad program strategies in a way that will be useful for human service practitioners. Chapters 4 through 10 include numerous examples of actual programs, followed by a discussion of professional roles and practical issues for human service practitioners to consider in planning and conducting network interventions.

The intervention projects selected for inclusion represent our comprehensive review of programs implemented throughout the country by private and public agencies at federal, state, and community levels. These programs, which attempt to enhance the social supports of the elderly, make innovative use of available personnel and fiscal resources and exhibit flexible approaches in intervening to meet human needs. Many of the projects described are still in the development and testing stages, and their efficacy cannot be evaluated fully. For some, effects on client satisfaction and reduced rates of institutionalization are reported. Together they represent stimulating and creative approaches to intervention in the social networks of the elderly and provide practical guidelines for personnel who are attempting to implement such models.

FINDING MODEL PROGRAMS

Our methodology for the collection of such material from around the country was extensive. We began with the assumption that innovative, creative programs to strengthen the support systems of the elderly already existed in the field, and that information about actual projects would be enriching to human service personnel working with the aging. Therefore, one of our initial tasks was to collect data from as many sources as possible that would describe existing projects and the materials they utilized for assessment, intervention, and evaluation. We contacted state aging agencies, major university aging and research centers, major national gerontological organizations, foundations with significant aging interests, and special aging projects. We also conducted a comprehensive computer-assisted review of published and unpublished literature. A special effort was made to access current or recent material about demonstration projects and model programs that were not likely to be available from published sources.

The result was a wonderful wealth of material drawn from projects from around the country, reflecting responses to specific needs discerned on the local, state, or federal level. Although we did not obtain information on every relevant project in the country, we received information on a wide range of projects dispersed over many different geographical areas. There are a wide variety of efforts to find solutions to problems. Agencies chose different strategies of intervention and focused on different client groups (i.e., the elderly themselves, the families of the elderly, other community helpers, etc.). The types of programmatic interventions also varied, involving different objectives, strategies, and emphases.

In order to make this wealth of information available and useful to the agency worker, a conceptual scheme was needed to identify and explain the network intervention strategies that were used, to make clear appropriate roles for agency staff, and to present issues for agency staff to consider in attempting to implement these interventions. The framework presented in the following section is used to organize the presentation of intervention modalities in Chapters 4 through 10.

ANALYZING NETWORK INTERVENTIONS

CONCEPTUALIZATION OF INTERVENTIONS

There have been a number of attempts at conceptualizing social network interventions in social welfare (Froland, Pancoast, & Chapman, 1979; Maguire & Biegel, 1982; Pancoast & Chapman, 1982; Trimble, 1980). The framework used here was developed by Biegel (in press).[1] Seven types of social network interventions are identified: clinical treatment, family caregiver enhancement, case management, neighborhood helping, volunteer linking, mutual help/self-help, and community empowerment (see Figure 3).

The distinctions made here between the types of network interventions oversimplify reality. In actuality, they represent analytically separable rather than discrete categories. Interventions in practice often utilize multiple network strategies. There is a separate chapter on mutual aid/self-help groups, as well as a section of the family caregiver enhancement chapter that deals with self-help groups. This is because the family caregiver enhancement category has as its primary focus a client group rather than a single intervention strategy. It seemed useful to include it here also as a single category because it represents an easily identified and widely used intervention modality.

For each of these seven types of network intervention strategies, four salient defining variables have been identified:

(1) *client group*—an elderly individual, family caregivers, or elderly in the neighborhood.

(2) *helper type*—either informal helpers, which includes family, friends, neighbors, people with similar problems, volunteers, and others; or formal or agency helpers.

(3) *locus of help*—neighborhood, community, or nongeographic.

(4) *level of help*—the public health model of prevention is utilized to measure the level of help. P = Prevention (primary prevention), T = Treatment (secondary prevention), and R = Rehabilitation (tertiary prevention).

ROLES FOR PROFESSIONALS

The worker in the aging network who attempts to identify and strengthen support systems for the elderly must perform a number of different professional roles. Given that the distinguishing characteristics of the various intervention modalities are essentially related to the professional roles carried out in each modality, we have paid careful attention to the definition of the roles and to differentiation of the roles that are most central for each intervention modality.

The categories of professional roles most useful for work in the aging network—especially as these relate to the intervention modalities described in this book—include the following: Advocate, Consultant, Coordinator, Direct Service Provider, Facilitator, Initiator/Developer, Linker: Intrasystem, Linker: Intersystem, Manager-Administrator, Resource Provider, and Supervisor-Teacher (see Figure 4). These categories draw on previous work done by Zastrow (1981), Baer and Federico (1978), and Teare (1981).

Type of Network Intervention	Client	Helper Type	Locus of Help	Level of Help
Clinical treatment	An elderly individual	Professional helpers, family, neighbors, friends	Nongeographic	T,R
Family caregiver enhancement —Education and training —Mutual aid —Coordination	family members of	Family, neighbors, friends, and professional helpers	Nongeographic	P,T
Case management	An elderly individual	Agency staff and personal network	Neighborhood, Nongeographic	T
Neighborhood helping	At-large elderly in neighborhood	Natural helpers, role-related helpers (gatekeepers)	Neighborhood	P,R
Volunteer linking	An elderly individual	Volunteers	Neighborhood	P,T,R
Mutual aid/Self-help	At-large elderly in the neighborhood	People with similar problems	Neighborhood, community, or nongeographic	P,R
Community empowerment	At-large elderly in the neighborhood	Lay and professional helpers	Neighborhood	P,R

FIGURE 3: A framework of social network interventions with the elderly. P = Prevention; T = Treatment; R = Rehabilitation. Adapted from Beigel (in press).

Roles	Clinical	Family Caretaker	Case Management	Neighborhood Helping	Volunteer	Mutual Aid	Community Empowerment
				Intervention Modalities			
Advocate						X	X
Coordinator			X				
Consultant		X		X	X	X	X
Direct service provider	X						
Facilitator		X		X	X	X	X
Initiator-developer		X		X	X	X	X
Internetwork linker	X	X	X	X			X
Intranetwork linker	X		X	X			X
Manager			X		X		
Resource provider		X				X	
Supervisor					X		

FIGURE 4: Professional roles.

The functions of each role are as follows:[2]

(1) *Advocate:* Organizes activity designed to obtain goods, services, power, or other resources for client(s).

(2) *Consultant:* Provides guidance and assistance to the primary caregivers or service deliverers in order to help them perform at a higher level of functioning.

(3) *Coordinator:* Brings together a variety of formal services in order to provide more comprehensive, more cohesive, and/or more relevant services to the client(s).

(4) *Direct Service Provider:* Provides services of support, counseling, and marshalling resources directly for the client(s).

(5) *Facilitator:*Expedites the mobilization of services and/or activities for the client(s).

(6) *Initiator/Developer:* Creates, organizes, and mobilizes activities, programs, and services for client(s).

(7) *Linker: Intrasystem:* Brings together various components of the informal support systems to serve the client(s) better.

(8) *Linker: Intersystem:* Brings informal support systems into relations with the formal service systems to provide better service for client(s).

(9) *Manager-Administrator:* Oversees and handles the organizational details of services and resources so that they will perform adequately for the client(s).

(10) *Resource Provider:* Brings resources to the informal support system and/or helps to create these resources so that the informal support system can provide better services to the client(s).

(11) *Supervisor-Teacher:* Oversees the professional workers and assists them to perform more adequately by improving their knowledge and their skills; requires the worker to be accountable for performing the work as expected by the agency or organization.

Each role requires specific knowledge to be executed successfully. The knowledge that is basic to working in the field of aging, with a focus on informal support systems, includes the following knowledge areas: knowledge of aging processes, including biological, mental, social and emotional processes; knowledge of normal human growth and development; knowledge of community dynamics; knowledge of ethnicity and social class and their impact on human behavior; knowledge of relevent systems, resources, and services; knowledge of informal support systems and their dynamics; and knowledge of impact of change, loss, and grief on human functioning.

Some of these knowledge areas are basic for all professionals. However, in working in the aging field some specific emphases are necessary. For example, in looking at family systems of the elderly, the emphasis must be on the place of the older person within the system. When there is no family present, emphasis on the roles and functions of families helps the worker to assess the impact of the loss of family, so that substitute activities or programs may be devised to offset the losses of the family. Each knowledge area has a generic component, with a specialized component for work with older persons.

Skills are also important to delineate. As we have worked on this effort, we have clearly seen that the ways knowledge is applied differentially to the various intervention modalities require application skills that flow from the knowledge. These are not automatically present when the knowledge is gained. The skills required are essentially based in the professional roles and are enhanced by the knowledge. Thus a direct service provider must have the generic knowledge described above with some special emphasis on individual, family, and group dynamics. This worker must be able to carry out effectively the role functions whose components are incorporated into the descriptions of each role.

IMPLEMENTATION ISSUES

A variety of practical issues arise in any professional intervention. Based on our research, we identified the following variables as significant for consideration in planning and implementing interventions:

(1) Administrative support. As most human service practitioners work in agencies, a key issue to consider in any intervention attempt is this: Does the agency support the planned program? Administrative support has both tangible and intangible components. On an intangible level, it represents an agency recognition or commitment to the intervention such that it is clear to agency board and staff that this intervention is recognized, endorsed, and validated by the agency administrator. On a mcre tangible level, administrative support can be defined as the agency providing sufficient resources—including money, expertise, staff, and time—to implement the planned intervention adequately.

In our consideration of administrative support, we have identified two variables that are important for agency practitioners to consider in estimating

Type of Network Intervention	Change Quotient	Staff Time
Clinical treatment	M	H
Family caregiver enhancement:		
—Education and training	L	L
—Mutual aid	M	L
—Coordination	H	M
Case management	M	M
Neighborhood helping	H	M
Volunteer linking	M	M
Mutual aid/self-help	M	L
Community empowerment	H	H

FIGURE 5: Administrative support.

the degree of administrative support required for particular interventions to be implemented successfully. The first variable we have called the *change quotient* (see Figure 5). This variable represents a combination of the degree of change the intervention represents for the agency (this ranges from an intervention that is very similar to the agency's usual methods of service delivery; to an intervention that represents a somewhat different strategy from that of agency practice, which requires, for example, additional training for staff and/or reallocation of resources; to an intervention that represents a major departure from the way the agency's services are currently organized and delivered) and the degree to which the intervention is controversial and therefore liable to engender resistance from the agency board, administrator, staff, or community groups.

We have ranked the change quotient for each intervention type on a three-point scale from low (L) to high (H). Given that a particular intervention modality can consist of a variety of different program strategies, these rankings represent our best estimate of the average for each modality, taking into account variability in intervention strategies within each modality. The higher the change quotient, the more imperative it is to have the agency administrator's backing of the intervention if the project is to be successful.

The second variable is the resources required to conduct the intervention. Here we have chosen to focus on one particular resource, *staff time*, because personnel costs in human service agency budgets are typically over 80% of the total agency budget and therefore represent the most significant agency resource. Again, this variable has been rated for each intervention modality on a three-point scale from low (L) to high (H).

(2) Evaluative indicators. For each intervention modality, a number of evaluative indicators are presented (see Figure 6). The indicators are listed

Type of Network Intervention	Evaluative Indicators
Clinical treatment	—Number of elderly clients and number of caregivers —Demographic and socioeconomic characteristics of caregivers and elderly clients —Increase in number of network members —Increase in quantity of network involvement —Increase in quality of network involvement —Positive changes in elderly client
Family caregiver enhancement Education and training	—Number of caregivers involved —Demographic and socioeconomic characteristics of caregivers —Satisfaction of caregivers with program —Knowledge gained by caregivers —Decreased burden of caregivers —Increased social support of caregivers
Mutual aid	—Number of caregivers involved —Demographic and socioeconomic characteristics of caregivers —Continued participation of caregivers —Decreased burden of caregivers —Increased social support of caregivers —Increase in leadership responsibilities exercised by group members
Coordination	—Number of caregivers involved —Demographic and socioeconomic characteristics of caregivers —Establishment of treatment plan —Services given to caregivers —Changes in elderly individuals —Decreased burden of caregivers —Increased social support of caregivers
Case management	—Identification of unmet needs —Mobilization of resources for elderly —Increased internetwork linkages —Decreased fragmentation of services —Improvement in client functioning
Neighborhood helping	—Number of informal helpers —Demographic and socioeconomic characteristics of helpers —Number of elderly helped

FIGURE 6: Evaluative indicators.   (continued)

Type of Network Intervention	Evaluative Indicators
	−Demographic and socioeconomic characteristics of elderly −Increased services given to elderly −Unmet needs of elderly addressed −Increase in intra- and internetwork linkages
Volunteer linking	−Number of volunteers −Demographic and socioeconomic characteristics of elderly and nonelderly volunteers −Number of elderly and nonelderly served −Demographic and socioeconomic characteristics of elderly and nonelderly served −Retention of volunteers −Satisfaction of volunteers −Services given by volunteers −Needs addressed by volunteers −Satisfaction of elderly and nonelderly clients −Positive changes in elderly and nonelderly clients
Mutual aid/self-help	−Number of participants (elderly and informal helpers) −Demographic and socioeconomic characteristics of participants −Retention of group members −Increase of leadership responsibilities exercised by group members −Reduction of stress, loneliness of group members −Increase of social support of group members −Amount and types of service exchanges −Increase in functioning levels of elderly due to service exchanges or artificial networks
Community empowerment	−Number of participants −Demographic and socioeconomic characteristics of participants −Issues addressed −Changes in informal and formal systems −Increase in intra- and intersystem linkages −Increase in capacity of community to address unmet human needs

FIGURE 6:   Evaluative indicators.

in outline format and can be divided into two broad categories. The first grouping represents a description of *effort*—what was done—whereas the second represents the *outcome* (performance) of that effort—what was changed (Suchman, 1967). For each intervention modality, effort indicators are placed before outcome indicators.

(3) Obstacles and limitations. There is an old saying about "the best laid plans of mice and men." Interventions are easier to plan than to implement. If practitioners can anticipate potential implementation difficulties before they begin their intervention, some unanticipated problems may be overcome. In Figure 7, we have identified two sets of such potential difficulties, *obstacles* and *limitations*. Obstacles are defined as factors that may prevent, delay, or inhibit the development of a successful intervention. They thus represent a preintervention variable. Limitations, on the other hand, are a postintervention variable and represent factors that may cause an intervention that has been undertaken to be less successful or less widely applicable than planned. Once again, these variables are indicated on the chart in outline format. A small percentage of identified examples are both obstacles as well as limitations and have therefore been placed under each of these variables.

(4) Cautions. Although perhaps one learns best from one's mistakes, we offer a number of cautions to practitioners in Figure 8. Neither these cautions nor the obstacles and limitations cited above are meant to dampen or limit enthusiasm for network interventions. Rather, they are offered to assist practitioners to design the most effective interventions.

It is clear from the above discussions of the conceptualization of interventions, professional roles, and administrative issues, as well as an examination of Figures 3-8, that there is considerable variety in the methodology, roles, staff skill, and staff time required to conduct the seven types of network intervention. It is logical to inquire, then, about how one chooses a particular intervention. This is of particular concern when more than one intervention technique might be available to meet the needs of particular clients.

Choosing an appropriate network intervention technique is similar to the development of any intervention strategy. A careful assessment must be made of the strengths and weaknesses of the client's support system (as indicated in Chapter 2). Once this assessment is completed, the worker makes a professional judgment as to the most appropriate technique to utilize. This judgment takes into consideration the unmet needs and preferences of the client, as well as the resources and capabilities of the agency.

Type of Network Intervention	Obstacles	Limitations
Clinical treatment	−Time consuming −Reorientation of staff −Specialized skills needed −Difficulties in mobilizing support systems	−Time consuming −Expensive −Not feasible with all clients −Privacy issues −Fear of rejection by network −Can't address immediate issues
Family caregiver enhancement		
Education and training	−Variations in age and needs or problems of caregivers	−Burnout of caregivers −Family rivalries
Mutual aid	−Support services may be needed to allow caregivers to attend −Reluctance of individuals to join self-help groups	−Family rivalries −Not all people helpful to one another −Needs of all people in group not identical −Burnout of caregivers
Coordination	−Appropriate role of caregivers and staff −Redefinition of staff	−Family rivalries −Burnout of caregivers
Case management	−Confidentiality −Changed staff role −Appropriate role for informal helpers	−Pluralistic system difficult to coordinate −Gap and lack of services
Neighborhood helping	−Attitudinal and value differences between informal and professional helpers −Some informal helpers hard to identify	−Rivalries, turf issues −Hard to evaluate

	—Administrative support	—Not for problems requiring specialized skills
	—Accountability-productivity issues	or long-term commitments
	—Specialized skills needed	—Matching of volunteers and service recipients
Volunteer linking	—May be threatening to staff	
	—Administrative support	
	—Needs careful assessment	
	—Volunteers may be difficult to recruit for certain needs in certain communities	
Mutual aid/self-help	—Reluctance of particular individual to join self-help/service exchange programs	—Not all people helpful to others
		—Groups behavior may be destructive
		—Needs of all people in group not identical
Community empowerment	—Time consuming	—Time consuming
	—Administrative support	—Results long term
	—Funding	—Is not feasible in all agencies or all communities
	—Threatening	
	—Specialized skills needed	

FIGURE 7: Obstacles and limitations.

49

Types of Network Intevention	Cautions
Clinical treatment	—Specialized intervention not suitable for all staff or all clients
Family caregiver enhancement	
Education and training	—Balanced emphasis on knowledge and feelings
Mutual aid	—Professionals must not assume leadership roles —Destructive group members
Coordination	—Relationship of professional and informal systems —Payment to caretakers
Case management	—Professionals must recognize their role is coordinative, not direct practice —Professional agencies must not dominate informal resources
Neighborhood helping	—Professional intervention may weaken informal networks
Volunteer linking	—Should not be used as a substitute for staff cuts —Volunteers need to be integrated into total agency —Agency staff need to be involved in planning —Need for training and supervision
Mutual aid/self-help	—Professionals must not assume leadership roles
Community empowerment	—Need to focus on long-term process, not on short-term products —Professionals must abide by the community's right to "decide" —Avoid conflict for its own sake; avoid confusing tactics and ends

FIGURE 8:   Cautions.

Sometimes more than one technique can be used with a given client system. For example, a 70-year-old widow who lives alone may be helped by participation in a self-help group for widows; her daughter, who provides major caregiving responsibilities, may be helped by a caregiver-enhancement program.

The worker's assessment of the needs of the relevant support system(s), from which elderly persons can or may draw their strengths, must always have a multifaceted lens through which to examine what *is*, what *needs* to be, and what *can* be. This multifaceted approach increases the range of the possible, an important aid in enhancing the life quality of elderly persons. The following chapters apply this lens to guide workers in their selections of suitable modalities.

EXERCISES AND STUDY QUESTIONS

1. Pick three problems of the elderly in your own or your agency's caseload that can be addressed by social network interventions.
2. For each problem, answer the following questions:
    a. Which type of network intervention would you utilize? Why?
    b. What professional roles would workers utilize?
    c. What difficulties do you anticipate in developing this intervention? How can these difficulties be overcome?
    d. How would you evaluate this intervention?

NOTES

1. The Biegel framework is an expansion and revision of the pioneering efforts of Charles Froland and Diane Pancoast, who developed the first conceptualization of social network interventions.

2. In the following definitions, client refers to the unit of attention, which may be the individual, family, group, or community organization.

SUGGESTED READINGS

Biegel, D. (in press). The application of network theory and research to the field of aging. In W. J. Sauer & R. T. Coward (Eds.), *Social support networks and the care of the elderly: Theory, research, practice and policy.* New York: Springer.

Pancoast, D. L., & Chapman, N. J. (1982). Roles for informal helpers in the delivery of human services. In D. Biegel & A. Naparstek (Eds.), *Community support systems and mental health: Practice, policy and research.* New York: Springer.

Zastrow, C. (1981). *The practice of social work.* Homewood, IL: Dorsey Press.

Chapter 4

CLINICAL TREATMENT

As we have noted in Chapter 1, individuals' responses in crises depend on the nature of the stress, their current coping strengths, and the quality of the affective and aid-oriented assistance provided by their social network. This third variable, social support, we see as a buffer, enhancing the coping capacity of individuals and allowing them to remain healthy even in the face of considerable stress. Some of these salient issues warrant a recapitulation for this modality, to distinguish it from other types of clinical treatment.

Interaction with trusted others is thus essential to well-being throughout life and perhaps takes on even greater significance in old age, when coping strength may be reduced and stresses increased. As noted earlier, there is a continuum of loss experienced in aging relating to sensory functioning, mental functioning, income, self-image, self-esteem, control, power, and kin and kith supports. Elderly may experience loss of elasticity in the ability to bounce back after an illness or crisis.

Like all of us, the elderly need others for survival. These significant others may be family, friends, relatives or neighbors on whom the elderly naturally and differentially rely. More casual relationships with neighbors, mail carrier and grocers, for example, also contribute to maintaining a network of social support for the elderly individual. There is some evidence that different types of networks are useful for solving different kinds of problems. Some research has shown that tight-knit, small networks (i.e., family networks) tend to aid in emotional concerns, whereas larger networks with looser ties (acquaintance networks) are more helpful in situations in which specific instrumental help, not usually available from close friends and relatives, is required (Wellman, 1981).

Clinical treatment based on a social network approach thus stresses the centrality of an individual's support system to his or her mental health and daily functioning. As Germain and Gitterman (1980) make clear in the "Life Model" of social work practice, people's needs and problems are located in the interface between person and environment. A social network approach takes an ecological perspective that focuses dually on intrapsychic change within the individual and changes within the person's social environment. The role of the mental health professional in this intervention accordingly involves assessment of the client's situation from a social systems viewpoint, rather than solely from an intrapsychic point of view.

The clinical treatment approach involves assisting clients by intervening with their social support networks. The primary goal is to increase the support provided by the network and direct it toward meeting the specific unmet affective and instrumental needs that are the focus of concern. A number of different strategies for such intervention with clients' networks can be utilized. Clients' existing networks may be *strengthened*. The worker's goal would be one of supporting and encouraging the relationships and assistance already intrinsic to an existing network. Alternatively, a worker may work toward *expanding* the support provided by the existing network by encouraging members to take on increased, broader functions or by drawing individuals on the network's periphery into more central helping roles. A third approach, appropriate for those clients whose existing networks of support are limited or even essentially nonexistent, involves *creating* a network of supports for the client by developing linkages with others that did not exist previously.

The process by which the worker intervenes in clients' networks so as to strengthen the affective and instrumental support received from them involves a series of stages, irrespective of which eventual strategy is selected. Maguire (1983) identified the three stages as *identification, analysis,* and *linking.* The first two stages focus on developing an understanding of the existing social network of the client, including its size, basis of relationships, capacities, resources, and members' frequency of contact and willingness to help. The third stage involves the often creative process of linking the client with appropriate network members, and it is here that either strengthening, expanding, or creating network links is chosen as the appropriate strategy. In this stage, worker and client typically work together to decide whom to involve in helping and the ways in which these individuals will be involved.

Two distinct modalities of clinical treatment based on network intervention are in evidence in the literature. Although both are based on seeking solutions to clients' needs within their social networks, the actual procedure workers use and the roles taken differ. In the first approach, the workers' goals are accomplished by working with clients on the identification and analysis of their networks. Taking the structure of the networks into consideration, professionals then move into the linking stage by deriving a plan for using the social networks on clients' behalf, working with individual network members to elicit their support and cooperation with the treatment plans devised. This modality has been used widely with different age groups in diverse settings.

The second approach is seen less frequently in the literature and involves the direct participation of the social network to a much greater extent. The network members identified by a client—family, friends, neighbors, coworkers, and relevant professionals—are convened in a series of "network sessions." There they work together, further analyzing the client's network, discussing the client's difficulties, and arriving at a viable plan of action in which they will themselves take part. Members indicate what they feel would be needed for the client and the part they would be willing to play in meeting the client's needs. In this approach, the linking stage of arriving at an appropriate treatment strategy is shared by the client's entire network. Workers using this modality function more as facilitators and catalysts for the involvement and activity of the informal network, than as primary planners and problem solvers.

Both of the above clinical treatment modalities have been used with elderly clients. A number of examples of such clinical interventions are described below. The first two exemplify the more usual approach of workers working with clients and social network members. The third example describes a program that involves the convening of network sessions on behalf of elderly clients.

PROGRAM EXAMPLES

Swenson (1979) cites an example of a social network intervention with an elderly client using the more typical approach to working with networks. This example illustrates the potential for meeting clients' needs in an innovative fashion by intervening in their support systems. In the situation described, an evaluation of the condition of an isolated woman, who was highly suspicious of her neighbors, and who had lived in the same apartment for 36 years, led community mental health center staff to decide to build on the strengths of an existing relationship between the client and her building superintendent. This man, who had made the original contact with the center because of his concern for the client, had been consistently eager to help. He was known to visit the client, take her to the doctor, and remind her to fix her lunch. The center staff decided on support of the superintendent as the principal intervention and offered him emotional support and professional backup to continue doing what he was already doing well. The social worker visited this man at his building and dropped in to see the elderly client at the same time. Swenson reports this strategy as having continued satisfactorily at the time of her article, over a year after it was initiated.

Cohen and Sokolovsky (1981) report on a clinical intervention with the elderly that is also based on the worker intervening in the client's network. This technique developed out of their research with elderly people in single-room occupancy (SRO) hotels. The tenants in these hotels have a range of mental, physical, and social problems. They typically have great needs, but they mistrust and therefore underutilize professional services.

The authors developed a tool, the "Network Analysis Profile," to analyze the social networks of these individuals. The instrument has both research and therapeutic applicability. It charts the interaction among various components of the resident's personal network (i.e., tenant-tenant, tenant-kin, and tenant-agency staff). Among variables examined for each interaction are content of the relationship and frequency, duration, intensity, and directional flow of the links.

This profile is described as being very useful at both the agency and the client level. At the agency level it can sensitize agency personnel to the strengths of even the most isolated of population groups. It can also assist staff to understand human behavior within a systems framework; and it can help the agency allocate staff resources to those individuals most at risk. Finally, it can help the agency personnel establish relationships with natural helpers identified by the instrument.

At the client level, the instrument can be completed with the standard intake forms used by a service agency. The resultant information can help the agency identify individuals at high risk and can assess the strengths and weaknesses of an individual's social network.

Once the worker has obtained this information, interventions can be planned through this network. According to Cohen and Sokolovsky (1981), before workers intervene professionally to help clients solve problems or meet needs, they see if help is available from caregivers in the client's network. Also, workers assess whether any professional services being planned have a negative impact on the assistance already provided through the network. For example, if an agency offers a loan to a client, it may harm the client's relationship with a neighbor who provides not only a loan but also social support and companionship. An additional role of the professional is to assess the fragility of the network; for example, whether the client was relying on one particular person whose loss might be devastating. Should analysis of the social network reveal individuals who had significant needs not being met by their informal network, the professionals should create networks either targeted to one individual or on a group level targeted to a number of at-risk individuals.

Cohen and Sokolovsky's (1981) work also included an experimental study of their network intervention technique, which helped to identify impediments and limitations of its use. In this study two social workers in an SRO hotel sought to deal with problems raised by tenants through network procedures wherever possible, rather than by the direct assistance of project staff. Records were kept as to whether network interventions were attempted and, if so, whether they succeeded or failed.

A total of 156 residents, approximately half of whom were aged 60 or over, presented over 500 problems. The five most common problem areas were emotional support, physical health, income, hotel conditions, and information and advice. Overall, at least one network intervention was attempted for 75% of the sample. Of these, 19% were dealt with successfully through a network procedure. Of those problems that were treated with a network approach, two-fifths had successful outcomes, and one-third of the sample experienced at least one successful network intervention. For certain problem areas such as sustenance, new housing, and advice, there were higher success rates, whereas for drug and employment problems there were low success rates. These results suggested to the authors that at least for some population groups, the initial enthusiasm that network intervention could serve as an alternative to direct service delivery had to be tempered. However, it was indicated that there needed to be further specification as to the types of problems appropriate for intervention based solely on network mobilization. This is especially true in the case of individuals whose natural networks are severely limited as to the number and type of individual members.

As a result of this study, Cohen and Sokolovsky identified several key factors as impediments to network interventions:

(1) Trust: Many residents were reticent about discussing their personal networks with social workers.

(2) Perceived isolation: Individuals appeared unaware of the supportive nature of their social interactions.

(3) Support systems may have been utilized or exhausted prior to coming to the worker for assistance.

(4) Certain areas (e.g., money) were considered private matters that, clients felt, could be discussed only with an "official" person such as a social worker.

(5) Problems frequently had to be dealt with immediately, and this did not allow sufficient time for work to be done with the network.

A third clinical intervention technique, developed by Garrison and Howe (1976), relies on "network sessions" as described above. The authors indicate the goals of their intervention as twofold: to modify the network of emotional influences (affective resources) of the client so as to promote active coping with the problems, and to articulate the needed instrumental resources represented by formal services. These goals are reached by convening network sessions, guided by the clinician and attended by the elderly client and all significant members of his or her network.

Five essential components of the network session have been identified by the authors: defining the client's problem as specifically as possible, listing alternative courses of action, listing liabilities and assets for each alternative, deciding on an alternative and testing it, and evaluating outcome, which may involve an additional session to permit feedback. These network sessions have included from 5 to 30 persons and have lasted from one to three hours. Clients typically participate in two or three sessions spaced from two to eight weeks apart.

Garrison and Howe present a case example that illustrates the use of their intervention technique. In this case, a man approached a local mental health center for help with his 72-year-old mother. His mother, married for 50 years to her 75-year-old husband, had recently undergone two operations. Although physically recovered from both, she was regressing into a serious psychological and physical dependency in which she was not eating well, was withdrawn and depressed, complained of pain, and spent most of her time in bed. A brief psychiatric hospitalization proved to be of no help.

The mental health worker proposed that a network session be held to discuss potential solutions with his mother and the important people in her life. The worker helped the family make a list of all the significant people in the patient's life at that time. These included the patient and her husband, their son, the daughter-in-law, two grandchildren, two of the parent's aunts, four card game partners, and a physician. Except for the family doctor (who agreed to be available by telephone if needed), these people agreed to attend the session, described to them "as a problem-solving session where we will all put our heads together to help get Mrs._____ back on her feet.''

In the network session the professional led the group in a discussion of the problem, and potential solutions were elicited from the group. Everyone agreed that the patient had to become active again; several people offered support and specific plans. After much negotiation between the patient and various members of her social network, a number of specific commitments were made, which included the patient's agreeing to play cards at her friend's home, for which her aunt would provide transportation, and several people planning to call daily to check on progress and provide encouragement. The patient also agreed to start cooking lunch again if her husband would accompany her for walks. Follow-up sessions at two weeks and six months indicated that the plan was working; the client was functioning at her preillness level by the latter session.

In contrast to this particular case, the network sessions with elderly clients frequently included several service professionals representing various resources, the authors indicate. For example, the network session for an elderly client with impairment due to chronic brain syndrome included a nurse and two rehabilitation counselors, who are described as having been invaluable in helping the client and family plan a home management program. When no relatives are available, sessions may include neighbors, the building janitor, or social companions of the clients. Cohen and Sokolovsky indicate that such social network intervention seems particularly well suited as a clinical approach with elderly clients who often experience problems that benefit from a coordinated multiple-person effort to meet both affective and instrumental needs.

SUMMARY:
PROGRAM EXAMPLES—CLINICAL TREATMENT

—Interventions of the clinical treatment modality involve increasing the social support provided by the client's network and directing it toward meeting unmet instrumental and affective needs of the client.

—Such intervention may entail *strengthening* an individual's existing support network, *expanding* that network, or *creating* a support system where one previously did not exist.

—Two distinct approaches to clinical treatment are noted. The first involves the worker using the network on the client's behalf, working with network members to elicit their involvement in the client's treatment.

—The second approach involves the actual convening of the members of an individual's network into a "network session" directed toward working together to create a treatment plan, developed and sponsored by the network members themselves.

—The professional role of the worker is noted to differ in the two approaches. In the first the worker has a more directive planning function; in the second the role is more of a catalyst facilitating the network members' task of deriving a workable treatment plan.

—The program examples included in this chapter indicate that both clinical treatment approaches have been effective in working with elderly clients.

PROFESSIONAL ROLES

The roles that are relevant to clinical intervention are direct service provider, internetwork linker, and intranetwork linker. In the provision of direct service, workers use their relationships with client(s) in direct interaction with the client(s). This use of relationship includes performing an assessment of the needs and resources that are available. These resources include the client's personal resources, including the ability to function physically, mentally, and emotionally—plus the ability of the support system to provide emotional support, care, and tangible resources. The personal resources of the client are called "coping capacities" in this conceptual framework (Mechanic, 1982, 1978). They are also useful to think about as the person's survival skills (or competencies).

Older persons' losses of both supports and coping capacities may be great, so the clinical intervener must pay extra attention to providing supports and resources. This attention is also necessary because of the characteristic sudden changes in functioning of older persons. If workers are not alert, quick deterioration that becomes irreversible may occur. The overload of losses older people experience often is the precipitating factor in the loss of ability to cope and is compounded by the fact that many of these losses are in the informal support system. This can create such burdens that the support system cannot continue to function. To recognize or anticipate changes and to intervene by direct emotional support, as well as by provision of resources and mobilization of resources, is an essential aspect of effective clinical intervention.

In addition to providing the relationship of worker to client as a resource, the clinical worker must be able to link the relevant formal systems to the elderly persons so that they are brought together into a cohesive plan for the use of elderly persons and their support systems. Clinical workers must also link between the client's informal systems so that they can be made aware of each other's roles and learn to work together better. Often there are informal helpers concerned with a client or client group that do not know of each other's presence or interest. Clinical workers must identify all interested persons, and often can help to bring them together to provide supports to one another so that they then can provide better support to the older person.

IMPLEMENTATION ISSUES

ADMINISTRATIVE SUPPORT

We have presented two differing intervention techniques in the program examples section above. In the first, as we have seen, the worker helps clients to identify individuals in their networks who may play supportive roles, and then the worker acts to facilitate the strengthening of network ties. The change quotient for this technique is moderate because it may involve somewhat of a change from usual agency practice. Often clinical interventions with the elderly are more psychodynamically focused and do not involve explicit, well-developed strategies to assist the individuals by strengthening their ties with significant others. However, such an approach is often accepted more readily by staff and therefore produces little resistance. The second technique, convening network members, represents a high change quotient. This technique is highly specialized, requires significant training, and is not suitable or intended for all clients. Staff resistance is likely to be higher than with the first technique because of the perceived general unsuitability of this technique in most agencies. Staff time in both techniques is high because this intervention modality involves one-to-one interaction with a client (or client system) as opposed to other techniques in which groups of clients are worked with at the same time.

EVALUATIVE INDICATORS

To evaluate the effectiveness of this technique, one should examine, on an *effort* level, the number and characteristics of elderly clients and network members served. On an *outcome* level, it is important to measure the increase (if any), on both qualitative and quantitative levels, of the involvement with the elderly client. Finally, workers should determine if elderly clients have experienced positive change as a result of clinical network intervention. It is important also to examine cases where change is not positive in order to determine particular problem areas or types of clients for whom the intervention is not effective. This, in turn, indicates whether a change in intervention techniques should be made, or if the intervention should be limited in scope to particular problems and/or directed to particular clients.

OBSTACLES AND LIMITATIONS

A number of obstacles may make this intervention modality difficult to undertake. Depending on which of the two major techniques are chosen, the intervention may require reorientation of staff and highly specialized skills. As we have said, both techniques are time-consuming. The worker may also experience difficulty in mobilizing support systems of particular clients. Some persons in the informal system may not see themselves as part of the client's network or may not wish to become involved. On one hand, workers should show persons in the support system how important their support is to the client; on the other hand, they should make sure that potential network members do not become overburdened with demands they cannot meet.

There may also be a number of limitations. Some clients may resist involving their network members, particularly asking their children for help. Workers should spend sufficient time to work through clients' resistance to having the family contacted. The appropriate response of the worker depends on the cause of the resistance. Sometimes this can be done by reassuring clients that their children care (if they do), given that the resistance is often based on fear of rejection. Sometimes clients have to be helped to deal with their fear of loss of control. They may need to be reassured that the worker will help them to maintain as much control as possible. Sometimes they need to deal with deep-seated feelings about accepting help, with the worker's help and guidance in eliciting these feelings. The worker's effort is focused on helping clients to work on the relevant issue(s) that may be producing or supporting some of the current estrangement and isolation.

Other clients, because of ethnicity, personal values, or for reasons of "privacy" may not want to have members of their network contacted or involved. The worker should evaluate the situation to see if the client's need for privacy is a shield to hide fear of rejection by network members, and must then assess the reality of this fear.

An additional limitation is that clinical network intervention may not be a feasible technique for addressing crisis issues. If the client has a pressing need, the worker should become directly involved and offer service because it might be too time-consuming to work through the client's network. A final limitation is that the second intervention technique, "the network session," is neither designed nor suitable for all clients. Therefore the worker must assess clients carefully for participation in this intervention technique.

CAUTIONS

One of the significant problems in the application of this methodology is the issue of the appropriate role of staff in dealing with both problems of the individual and problems of the informal support system. It is difficult to avoid tending to either blame or be critical of family and/or the individual client when the necessary support is not forthcoming. This is true for all of the network intervention methodologies, but in this particular approach there is often more substantial involvement by the worker in an one-to-one relationship with the client and the family. One of the best antidotes for this problem is developing a family-centered or system-centered approach that helps to avoid identification of any one person in the system as the culprit or victim. Once this interactional view begins to develop, it is more possible to see the interactional factors as essential issues of concern. Training with staff is often necessary to develop and enhance this approach.

EXERCISES AND STUDY QUESTIONS

1. An elderly woman has been referred for service to your agency by her neighbor. She lives alone in a highrise apartment building, is increasingly unable to take care of herself, and her neighbors are worried that she might fall and hurt herself. The woman does not want to change her living status, preferring to remain in her own apartment. You believe that although she is somewhat fragile, she might be able to function adequately in her apartment if she had an enhanced ongoing support system. Using the clinical treatment approach, how would you help this woman? What steps would you take to assess her support system and to strengthen it? Whom would you involve and why?

2. What can the worker do if potential support system members do not want to become involved in helping a client?

3. How can the worker help support system members from becoming overburdened?

4. What can the worker do if a client does not want members of his or her network contacted?

SUGGESTED READINGS

Cohen, C. I., & Sokolovsky, J. (1981) Social networks and the elderly: Clinical techniques. *International Journal of Family Therapy, 3,* 281-294.

Garrison, J. E., & Howe, J. (1976). Community intervention with the elderly: A social networks approach. *Journal of the American Geriatrics Society, 24,* 329-333.

Maguire, L. (1983). *Understanding social networks.* Beverly Hills, CA: Sage.

Chapter 5

FAMILY CAREGIVER ENHANCEMENT

This chapter focuses on intervention strategies whose target is the caregiver of the aged person. As such, it differs somewhat from the other strategies in our typology, which are differentiated primarily by the methodology of the intervention type. In this chapter, *client group* is the factor determining inclusion in this intervention category. Programs whose goals are to assist the caregivers of the elderly are included for discussion here.

A diversity of research has established the primacy of family members as caregivers of the elderly. As noted earlier, Brody (1977) estimates that 70%-80% of supportive care to older persons is provided by adult children. Gurland et al. (1978) found that 70% of the care received by the dependent elderly in his sample came from the family. If restricted to primary care, defined as care considered critical to the maintenance of the older person at home, family contribution increased to 77% of the total. A Cleveland needs assessment survey of the elderly, conducted by the General Accounting Office (1977), revealed that family and friends provide over 50% of the services received by older persons at *all* levels of functioning, and over 79% for those who are extensively impaired. It appears that the more frail the elderly family member, the greater the likelihood that children will assume more responsibility for care (Nowak & Brice, n.d.)

Not surprisingly, it also appears that the family is the source of care preferred by the elderly. The New York State Office for Aging (1982), reviewing the literature, cites a study indicating that of approximately 400,000 older persons, kin—primarily children—emerged as the support element of first choice, followed by friends and neighbors, with formal organizations and people in miscellaneous other categories generally ranking last.

There has been increasing interest in the literature on the concept of family burden. Caregivers may experience a wide variety of problems when dealing with their family members, including emotional and financial strain, inconvenience, anxiety, depression, and balancing the demands of caregiving with other responsibilities deriving from family and work. Characteristics of the caregiver, as well as of the elderly family member, influence the quality of the relationship between the two and the degree of family burden that is felt (Gordon, 1981). The ages of involved persons, personalities, health status, and the long-term quality of their relationship have been found to influence this. Mental and physical symptoms such as severe memory loss or disorientation and urinary incontinence have been identified as especially likely to contribute to the degree of burden experienced. When family burden gets too great, a breaking point may be reached in which family members feel they can no longer cope, and institutional placement of the elderly person is sought. The decision to institutionalize the elderly family member has been found to be related more closely to the burden on families reaching unbearable proportions than to deterioration of the elderly person.

The intervention strategies addressed in this section involve intervening with the family caregivers of the elderly to lessen family burden. Strategies may involve either primary intervention in which the degree of family burden is prevented from becoming excessive, or may focus on secondary prevention that aims at reducing the negative effects of burden that have reached excessive levels. In either case, intervention with the family caregiver has implications for the well-being of elderly persons by raising the quality of care provided and improving the quality of the relationship between caregivers and elderly persons in order to increase the length of time elderly persons will continue to be cared for in the family setting. Program examples in this chapter are divided into three separate sections: *education and training, mutual aid/self-help groups,* and *coordination and formalization of services.* These approaches reflect both the extensiveness as well as the variety of modalities that can be used to support the family caregiver. Each section discusses a number of different program efforts.

EDUCATION AND TRAINING:
AN OVERVIEW

The rationale for programs for caregivers that stress educational and skill training as a major intervention mode is based on the role of basic knowledge in increasing the coping capacities of caregivers. Brice and Nowak (1982) describe this role:

> Basic knowledge, whether to increase awareness, develop technical skills, or learn to recognize, appropriately vent and self-manage emotional cues, dispels some of the fear and mystery about the events of late-life caretaking and replaces them with competencies, self-confidence and adaptive strategies for stress management in both personal and interpersonal contexts.

Programs of this type work to increase caregivers' technical caregiving skills and competency, and to furnish them with increased knowledge and understanding of issues associated with the aging process. The acquisition of knowledge and specific technical skills increases caregivers' "ability to cope with their aging family member, reducing the stress involved and increasing competencies in geriatric caregiving" (Brice & Nowak, 1982).

A variety of interventions in the educational and/or training mode have been described in the literature (Brice & Nowak, 1982; Office of Aging Studies, 1979; Zimmer, 1981). A number of these involve training projects that have been offered to caregivers. Others are in the form of printed training materials, such as curricula, pamphlets, and manuals, that represent available resources for program planning.

PROGRAM EXAMPLES

One well-developed training program was initiated in 1981 by the Center for the Study of Aging at the State University of New York at Buffalo. This project, entitled Caregivers Assistance and Resources for the Elderly's Relatives Series (CARERS), has as its goal reduction of stress and improvement of competencies through education of geriatric family caregivers. It is aimed at family members who are caring for an elderly relative, with particular interest in caregivers of elderly with some form of dementia or severe physical disability. Training foci include the basic processes of aging, practical caregiving skills, coping with the inevitable stresses of caring, and consumer advocacy in contracting for professional services. Specific skills are taught for handling relocation trauma and securing the physical environment.

CARERS consists of 13 two and one-half hour sessions held one morning a month. Cost to trainees is $5 per session. Trainees receive a certificate of completion issued by the University's Center for the Study of Aging on completion of eight different sessions, with strong encouragement to continue in the training sessions. An average of 30 persons per session have attended the program so far. A formal evaluation is reported to have been conducted recently by outside evaluators, but the results are not yet available (Brice & Nowak, 1982).

A shorter, six-hour training program offered to family caregivers and clergy was "Training to Enhance the Informal Support Systems of the Elderly." Its goals and content were similar to CARERS, focusing on increasing knowledge of aging processes, and increasing skills in working with the aged. This program, sponsored by the School of Social Welfare, Louisiana State University, was evaluated through a brief questionnaire given to participants at the end of the last training session, and also by means of a separate evaluation by the trainers. The trainees were found generally to express positive comments about the training. The training group was, however, smaller than anticipated, and attendance at the sessions was unpredictable (four-nine persons per session). The organizers of the program recommended that future sssions be longer to allow more time to discuss the content of the program and to allow the trainees to share their experiences. They also thought that more attention should be paid to the logistical details (transportation, day care, etc.) in order to reduce barriers to full participation (Office of Aging Studies, 1979, p. 21).

A widely used manual for replication of an educational program for adults with older parents or relatives is *As Parents Grow Older (APGO*; see Silverman et al., 1981). This manual was developed by the Institute of Gerontology at the University of Michigan in cooperation with Child and Family Services of Michigan, Inc. It outlines a program designed as a small group experience (10-12 members) for adults who have older parents or relatives and who are in need of some practical knowledge that will help them to understand their older relatives' changing needs.

The group sessions are meant to supply the caregiver with both information and social support in six two-hour sessions. The sessions include the following topics: increasing understanding of psychological aspects of aging; chronic illnesses and behavioral changes with age, sensory deprivation and communication, decision-making and alternative living situations, availability and utilization of community resources, and dealing with one's situation and feelings. The manual, which details curricula for each of these sessions, indicates that the information and materials were field-tested and evaluated in a number of Michigan communities. The *APGO* manual may be used as an information program only or, as the authors urge, as part of a more complete intervention process that provides for group involvement and discussion.

The New York State Office for the Aging has developed similar materials for a course for informal caregiving to the elderly entitled *Practical Help for Those Caring for an Elderly Person in the Community*. Like *APGO*, the course described involves six two-hour sessions that focus on increasing understanding of and abilities to cope with the caregiving situation. This course, developed in cooperation with the New York State Education Department, was reported to be pilot-tested at local schools. The testing led the authors to state that "evaluative evidence points to its usefulness and appropriateness of content for informal caregivers," although further information on the evaluation undertaken is not reported (New York State Office for the Aging, 1982, p. 1).

An additional type of educational program, focusing on printed materials rather than training programs or manuals for program development, was developed as a joint venture of the Cooperative Extension Service and the Gerontology Center of Pennsylvania State University. The methodology of this program, reported on by Smyer (1982), involved the preparation and distribution of six pamphlets covering various topics related to aging and family caregiving.

The goal of this program was for individuals to anticipate and prepare for the problems of aging they and their families will face and to become more aware of community resources. The pamphlets were available to the general community and were distributed through a self-referred list of 86 persons in a rural Pennsylvania county.

SUMMARY:
PROGRAM EXAMPLES—EDUCATION AND TRAINING
OF CAREGIVERS TO THE FRAIL ELDERLY

— Goal: reducing stress and increasing competencies of caregivers.

— These programs generally include education and training in the following areas: basic processes of aging; specific skills, such as stress management and patient care; and knowledge and utilization of community resources.

— Training programs appear to range from having 6-13 sessions, from one to two and one-half hours each. In addition, a program using printed materials rather than interactive training was noted.

— A number of different detailed training curricula in this area are available.

MUTUAL AND SELF-HELP GROUPS
FOR CAREGIVERS

Mutual help groups for the caregivers of the elderly, especially the frail elderly, have begun to emerge in many settings. Some are directed toward family members only and some include any interested individuals, including potential caregivers, family, and friends. There are groups organized for those who care for elderly family members with a specific diagnosis, such as senile dementia, and groups focused only on wives of disabled husbands. Groups have different emphases variously stressing information, emotional support, advocacy, or a combination of these. They may be self-directed with leadership coming from within the group, or may involve professional staff as group leaders or facilitators. It is noted that such issues are the same across the board for self-help groups with various clientele. Groups evidencing a particular structure often have a clear rationale for doing so, pointing to the benefits of such an approach. Examination of such rationales may be helpful to planners contemplating the development of self-help groups.

Developers of mutual aid groups for caregivers of the elderly have identified a number of reasons why such a strategy is likely to be suited to the needs of the caregivers. The Duke Family Support Program (Gwyther, 1982) identified four basic reasons:

(1) *Cultural ideology and experience:* In some cultures, family obligations for caring are willingly accepted as a personal responsibility, individuals prefer to assume responsibility for care as far as possible.

(2) *Social change:* The family is uncertain of its capacity to care for its members; associating with other families helps to create a sense of community.

(3) *Managing stigma:* Diseases and disorders that are poorly understood by professionals and lay persons are frequently stigmatizing. Caregivers have difficulty understanding their own thoughts and emotions and explaining these to others. They turn to those who, because of their similar experiences, are likely to understand.

(4) *Limitations of professional help.* Professionals acknowledge that they often do not understand totally what is involved in the management of chronic disorders and therefore have limited abilities to help with this task. Caregivers turn to each other for information about the techniques of coping with and surviving the demands of continual caregiving.

Mellor, Rzetelny, and Hudis (1981), discussing the Natural Supports Program of the Community Service Society, similarly stress the suitability of the self-help group approach for caregivers of the aged. They point out that caregivers are a recently identified population whose needs the professional service network is only just beginning to recognize, and that caregivers themselves often possess the necessary expertise and hold many of the solutions to their own problems. They also point out that caregivers of the aged are enmeshed in chronic, long-term situations that may worsen over time. This creates a need for continuing aid and support for the caregiver. A self-help group approach, they think, allows the continuation of a group for a long period of time.

Zarit and Zarit (1982) also indicate the advantage of the group in enabling caregivers to make suggestions to one another based on personal experience of what has been most successful. Such an approach can involve creative solutions to problems. They suggest that participants will often try something new when proposed by another group member and might not follow a professional's suggestions. Caregivers in support groups are also noted as modeling after one another; learning new strategies by observing what other participants did, particularly in areas where they previously had trouble making changes. They cite the case of one group in which some of the women caregivers were reluctant to bring help into the household to care for their husbands. The authors stated that the example set by the men in the group who used household help was instrumental in overcoming this reluctance.

PROGRAM EXAMPLES

The Natural Supports Program of the Community Service Society of New York has experimented with support groups for caring relatives in different types of communities (Getzel, 1981; Mellor, 1982; Natural Supports Program, 1981; Rzetelny & Mellor, 1981; Rzetelny et al., 1980; Zimmer, 1981). In one of these models, programs were developed initially as educational-informational sessions under professional leadership with one goal being their evolution into self-help groups run by the members themselves. Groups were responsible for deciding their own format, whether they were interested in emphasizing an educational format using speakers or concentrating on the mutual aid-peer support aspect. The extent of professional involvement was determined similarly by the interaction among members and depended on the willingness and ability of the members to assume responsibility and leadership for the group. The eventual goal was that groups would move to a total self-help model, with professional involvement limited to helping the group determine its initial structure and content. Help at later stages was to be limited to technical assistance. Assistance to group participants was offered by either arranging for or paying for both home care services and transportation to enable attendance at meetings without cost to the participants.

Results of an assessment carried out after the first year of operation of the National Support Program indicated four areas of need expressed by the caregivers: (1) *educational*—the need for information to provide an increased understanding of the aging process; (2) *didactic*—the need for skill training in the care and maintenance of a disabled older person and in the management of interactional family problems; (3) *emotional*—the need for recognition and support of the caring role; and (4) *concrete service*—the need for referral and information regarding resources. The findings also indicated several distinct groups of people whose needs might be addressed by a group program: those who anticipate assuming a caring role, those already providing care, those whose older relatives live far away, and those whose relatives live in institutions. On the basis of this exploration, the authors conclude that the group modality offers a unique opportunity for participants to share their concerns with others, engage in a process of mutual aid, develop skills for problem-solving and coping, facilitate problem definition, and clarify values and roles. A group modality, they also assert, offers an efficient way of disseminating information about services to many people simultaneously.

Another program aimed at interested individuals caring for an older person, or considering assuming this responsibility in the future, illustrates the potential for agency cooperation in such a venture. "Understanding the Older Person in Your Life/As Your Parents Grow Old" is a group discussion series administered by three agencies: The Cambria County Area Agency on Aging, Lutheran Social Services, and the Cambria County Cooperative Extensive Service of the Pennsylvania State University. With a public Area Agency on Aging, a private social service agency, and a state extension service involved, each is able to bring its unique capabilities to bear on program development and operation. A staff member from each of the three agencies contributes to the tasks of choosing discussion group leaders and providing overall program coordination. The Cambria County Cooperative Extension Service of the university publicizes the sessions in the *County Information and Educational Newsletter*. No funding is required for the program.

A number of the mutual aid group programs are aimed at caregivers of elderly persons with particular conditions. Notable among these are groups for relatives of seniors with senile dementia, a difficult condition especially disruptive of caregivers' lives. Among such programs are the Family Support Program of Duke University, Philadelphia's Aid to Caregivers of the Mentally Impaired Aged (ACMA), and the Pittsburgh Presbytery's program for providing support groups for caregivers.

The Duke University Program is an extensive state wide program establishing mutual aid groups throughout North Carolina. By 1982, over 1800 families were reported as being involved. In this program caregivers come to monthly meetings run by professional facilitators who volunteer a year's commitment to the mutual help group. The professional is a concerned individual who often also is a family caregiver.

The planners of the Family Support Program have stressed the importance of a central facility for the maintenance and extension of support groups, preferably the central facility of the state network. The program ensures the dissemination of current information, provides a telephone hotline, stimulates media interest, trains facilitators, and evaluates performance. Based on three years of program operation, the Family Support Program staff judged the mutual support groups as having been both therapeutic to caregivers and empowering for the community through the strengthening and mobilizing of community resources. A detailed assessment of the program is currently under way, although results have not yet been reported.

The ACMA program was started by the Philadelphia Geriatric Center in July 1982. It brings together family members caring for a relative with senile dementia into neighborhood support groups. Unlike the statewide Duke program, ACMA operates in the greater Philadelphia area developing groups on a neighborhood basis. Its eventual goal is to conduct 30 support groups throughout greater Philadelphia.

Like the model described in the Natural Supports Program above, the ACMA groups initially meet primarily as educational-informational sessions and then are assisted in becoming permanent self-help groups within the community. As with the previous model, leadership is assumed by an ACMA staff member for the first 10 weeks, which are devoted to educational objectives. This role is gradually transferred to group members, with the group having ongoing access to ACMA staff for consultation. An important aspect of ACMA is that participants also have access to supportive services such as sitter services, respite care, and a 24-hour hotline while they are in the program. Membership is free and open to any family member caring for someone with senile dementia.

The Pittsburgh Presbytery program recruits, trains, and supervises volunteer facilitators from churches who help organize and facilitate groups of family caregivers in each church. This effort has increased the number of caregivers getting support and has involved concerned volunteers in a supportive network.

There are also mutual aid groups for caregivers developed for those in specified relationships with the elderly individual, such as groups for adult children or for wives of disabled elderly. Women Who Care of Marin County, California is a support group organized for wives caring for disabled husbands. It was started by approaching women whose husbands were in an adult day program. Many of these women were originally reluctant to join, feeling that they would be taking on "one more burden in their already burdened lives." This initial reluctance was overcome, and the support group was begun.

Originally meeting on a monthly basis, the group was then scheduled to meet twice monthly at the request of the wives who wanted more time for educational programs of concern to them. The second meeting of the month was set aside for this purpose, resource people were invited to address such issues as preparing financially for a spouse's institutional care and the physical and psychological after-effects of a stroke.

The group involves a number of aspects that are seen as intrinsic to its success. Like ACMA discussed above, the program ensures that arrangements are made to care for husbands while the wives attend meetings. All meetings are held at the senior day care center, and husbands who do not normally participate may do so on meeting days.

The referral process entails some specific procedures that, in the opinion of group leaders, have enhanced its success. Women join the support group by way of referral from the day care program or other community agencies. Once referral is made, one of the coleaders contacts the woman to assess her individual situation and to explain the purpose and content of the group meetings. This is a vital step involving a new member, as it gives the coleader an opportunity to determine the level of supportive services the couple needs and helps the wife sort out which needs should be addressed first. She may, for example, need the respite provided by day care before she is able to focus on her own needs for emotional support. This contact also serves another important function in preparing the woman for the group process and the often emotionally charged issues that may be discussed. "It has been our experience," the leaders report, "that, without such an orientation, a woman is ill-prepared to deal with subject matter and intensity of feelings expressed in the meetings" (Crossman & Barry, 1981, p. 465).

After the coleader has spoken with the woman, one of the group members calls her. This outreach of the wives themselves is an important component of the process because it not only "increases the self-esteem of the group member but also provides a personal connection within the group for the new member." An additional report on this project points to the close collaboration of the mutual support group and its sponsoring agency as a factor in the group's success (Colman, Sommers, & Leonard, 1982, p. 9).

Through Women Who Care, the wives had an opportunity to share common experiences and explore alternative methods of coping and problem-solving. During this process they also received validation of their individual strengths and empathy and understanding for their negative feelings. The preventive function for the wives of such groups was also seen as important. In this group the majority of the wives themselves had at least one chronic health problem, and several suffered functional impairment as a result. For a few the stress of caretaking placed them in a particularly high-risk group.

A unique aspect of this group points to the potential momentum of such a program once it has been set into motion. The group successfully developed its own respite care project. During the first year of support group meetings, the women became increasingly concerned about the need for adequate, affordable respite service to relieve them of the daily demands of caregiving. They became their own advocates, and on discovering that local agency directors were sensitive to the problem but had no available funds, they wrote a grant proposal to a local foundation.

The result was The Wives Respite Project, a two-year program that included home care, overnight respite, and community-professional education. Funding for the program was obtained to enable these women to have the services they needed so badly and, in addition, was described as a powerful experience for them, validating their caregiving role and indicating that others recognized the enormity of their caregiving task. Their self-esteem is reported to have increased as a result—an important outcome for these women, many of whom experienced guilt over their difficulties in accepting, and inadequacy in dealing with, their multiple responsibilities.

SUMMARY:
PROGRAM EXAMPLES—
MUTUAL AID/SELF-HELP GROUPS FOR CAREGIVERS

— Support groups may be directed at a general audience, specified in terms of a relationship to an elderly individual (wives only, family members only) or in terms of the specific condition or diagnosis of the elderly person (senile dementia).

— The group may be focused on an educational and/or emotionally supportive approach. There is evidence that a combination of instrumental learning and opportunities for support and sharing of problems and solutions may be the most effective approach to meet caregivers' needs.

— Some programs alternate educational-informational meetings with those geared more toward group sharing. Another approach involves beginning a group with a series of educational-informational meetings after which a support group is encouraged to begin. The decision as to the group's format may be left up to the members themselves, determined by the professional staff, or may be a combination.

— An important issue in regard to these groups is that of group leadership: the combination of professional and lay staffing that will be involved. There appears to be valid arguments on both sides of the lay/professional leadership question. Fiscal concerns are likely to play a role in this decision. The more professional staff involved (unless on a volunteer basis), the more costly the program. One possibility apears to be starting the group under professional leadership and then moving to lay leadership with professional consultation available.

— The relationship and involvement of the sponsoring agency is also an important issue for support groups. Several programs have indicated the continued support and involvement of the sponsoring agency as an important element for success.

— The groups vary`in terms of the degree of preparation new group members receive. In some, interested parties simply come to meetings; in others they are first contacted by professional personnel or by other members who prepare them for the group and assess their suitability for membership.

— A number of the programs make provision for support services for members to facilitate their ability to attend meetings. These include respite care, transportation to meetings, or money to pay for "sitting" services and transportation.

FORMALIZATION AND COORDINATION
OF FAMILY CAREGIVING

An additional approach to the provision of support for the caregivers to the elderly involves recognition of the role of the family in caring for the elderly person and coordination of that role into an overall service plan. In this approach, the care the family is giving is determined and then often delineated formally within a service contract. The family's caregiving services may then be included in an overall plan of care for the elderly person with formal agency services used to meet the gaps in care. The agreed-on service package that details both informal and formal services to be used may then be described in a letter of agreement signed by all parties. Such programs may, in addition, involve paying for care provided within the family, thus implementing a policy recommendation suggested by Sussman (1976). Sussman argued for providing financial support to encourage and enable family members and neighbors to provide care to the elderly who would not otherwise be able to do so.

PROGRAM EXAMPLES

The Individual Services Component of the Natural Supports Program of the Community Service Society of New York was aimed at enhancing and strengthening informal supporters' efforts to continue providing care to disabled relatives (Getzel, 1981; Natural Supports Program, 1981; Rzetelny et al., 1980; Zimmer, 1982). This time-limited research and demonstration project was structured to provide counseling, information, referral, and "hard services" that enhance the caregiving role. The basic assumption was that families, friends, and neighbors are the "ultimate case managers"; that they have been providing care for a long time, that they know what and how much service is needed, and that the professional must support and enhance, not be a substitute for, their efforts. Families were therefore encouraged to define their own service package. The program was explicit in being concerned with not "pushing" services but rather in providing them when requested.

The procedure of the Individual Service Component, once eligibility was established, involved a family meeting that included the caseworker, the elderly person receiving care, and all those family members who gave care. This meeting served to determine the major disabilities of the older person, the nature and extent of family care provided, the family's definition of problems and stresses, and the services seen as helpful by the family in its caregiving role. Together they designed a service package that was geared at supplementing, not substituting for, family-provided care. One relative, identified as the primary natural support, was considered the case manager. A letter of agreement confirmed the nature of the family supports that would continue to be provided, as well as the agreed-upon service package offered by the program. Regular contact was maintained, and services could be altered as needs changed.

This intervention approach and sequence is described as emphasizing three tasks: (1) to aid family members to extend and/or continue their specific caregiving efforts on behalf of elderly relatives; (2) to acknowledge and credit caregivers as they encounter stresses brought on by caregiving, family pressures, and reactions to the elderly's changing condition; and (3) to mediate troubled family relations originating from caregiving. The agency provided services that were directed to these needs.

By April 1981, over 120 families had been served by this program. The service requested most frequently was some form of home care for the elderly person (personal care, household chores, or a combination of these). Also requested were respite care and counseling for the caregiver and/or elderly person.

In providing service to these families, the caseworker was called on to adapt services to the individual family patterns, often in a more flexible fashion than the system provided for—that is, home care in less than four-hour units or adjustments for a working daughter's schedule. Families were observed to respond positively to this and noted especially that this was the first time that their role and their needs were recognized.

Some evidence of the flexibility of service is evidenced in a case example of a childless couple; the wife's 90-year-old mother lived with, and was cared for, by them. The Natural Supports Program, responding to the daughter's request for respite, provided the couple with a monthly allowance, which they used for evening relief. The couple was described as enjoying their evenings out together and finding they were better able to balance their different roles.

A number of states have adopted similar approaches incorporating family caregiving with services provided by other sources, both formal and informal. This has involved, at times, paying relatives for care (State of Maine, 1983; State of Kentucky, 1982).

Home Based Care, the program of the Department of Human Resources of the State of Maine, provided in-home services to at-risk elderly. Developed specifically to serve the elderly at risk of institutionalization, Home Based Care involved an assessment of the elderly person and provision of services to meet their specific needs. The service that received the greatest amount of funding (42%) was personal care assistance, which included assistance with routine activities of daily living, such as dressing, bathing, toileting, food preparation, and other in-home tasks. Similar to home health aides, assistants offered great flexibility in schedules and costs. Only 4.5% of personal care assistance services were purchased from agencies; the rest were provided by people from the community, often families, neighbors, and friends of the clients.

The Department of Human Services concluded that Home-Based Care funds provided the family with those services they could not otherwise have obtained. Situations were noted in which the family care provider would otherwise not have been able to remain at home because of financial considerations. The program was structured, however, so that funding to families or neighbors was provided only when all other resources were exhausted. In this way, previous maintenance of effort was assured.

The department gave the following case example, which illustrates this approach:

> Mr. E, 79 years old, a severe arthritic with Alzheimer's Disease, needs two people to help him out of bed. He is incontinent and requires assistance with all activities such as bathing, eating and dressing. His wife, 76 years old, is a diabetic, had a stroke resulting in partial paralysis and has oxygen periodically for respiratory distress. The granddaughter gave up her job and with assistance from her husband and other family members, has been the primary caregiver of both grandparents since last March, for which she is being paid $100 per week. They continue to do well at home, with Mr. E showing some improvement recently. (State of Maine, 1983, p. 2)

It was found that of 521 clients served under the program (as of January 1983), 43 family members were reimbursed as primary care givers. Daughters were paid most frequently, with granddaughters also frequently involved as the primary care provider. Payments ranged from $25 to $175 weekly, with the median $100/week. In describing the clients served, 71% were over age 75, 69% were eligible for an intermediate care facility or skilled nursing facility care; and the remaining 31% were considered likely candidates for boarding home care. Of those served, 5% were in nursing homes and were able to return to their homes and families.

The Department of Human Services states that home-based care is a cost-effective alternative to the provision of nursing home care. The program has been evaluated through a family and client satisfaction questionnaire, and the results have been very positive. Additional evaluative mechanisms are needed to permit an assessment of the cost-effectiveness of this effort.

SUMMARY: PROGRAM EXAMPLES— FORMALIZATION AND COORDINATION OF FAMILY CAREGIVING

— These intervention strategies recognize and support family caregiving and incorporate it into a system of services that supplement, rather than substitute for, the family's involvement with the elderly individual.

— A number of these approaches involve a formal contract or letter of agreement between the family and the agency in which their respective service delivery roles are specified and formalized. A number also involves the paying of informal caregivers such as family, neighbors, and friends for their services so that these are supported and continued.

— The success of these interventions is flexibility in approaches that are not inhibited by bureaucratic agency regulations or procedures.

— Flexibility of staff and use of financial resources have been noted as critical in such approaches. The Natural Supports Program indicates in this regard that "of utmost importance is a flexible staff, knowledgeable and adept at mobilizing the resources in a community, who have no need to 'hang on' to individual cases or modalities, but who can work together in a supportive manner. In addition, there is a belief by staff in the basic strength and integrity of these families" (Rzetelny et al., 1980, p. 17). Staff must also be prepared to work non-traditional hours when necessary to meet families' needs.

— The innovative approach to paying family members to provide in-home care for the elderly has potential that is now being tested. Such programs entail nontraditional approaches to family responsibility, fiscal support, and use of monetary resources.

— Commitment at high administrative levels and administrative support of personnel and programs are critical elements in permitting and encouraging unorthodox use of staff time and fiscal resources.

PROFESSIONAL ROLES

The family caregiver intervention modality includes the professional roles of consultant, facilitator, initiator-developer, internetwork linker, and resource provider. The worker essentially serves as a consultant to the family caregiver(s) providing direct service to the elderly. The consultant role includes providing information about the processes of aging, both the normal processes and the specific ones occurring with this particular elderly person. The consultant also provides information about services, thus offering support, encouragement, and help with problem solving. The important focus here is that of being a helper to the primary caregiver. The worker must guard against taking over the caretaking responsibilities from the informal caregiver.

The facilitator is supportive of the family caregiver. This support is carried out through helping caregivers to know about resources; to connect with those resources, as needed; to provide emotional and physical supports directly to the caregiver; and to work with all other members or potential members of the informal support system so that they can play a more active role in supporting and relieving the caregiver.

The initiator-developer role arises in the creation of supports for the family caregivers such as classes, mutual help/self-help groups, and support for the development of needed services, including adult day care or respite care.

The role of internetwork linker is important because the worker must mobilize as many agencies and organizations in the formal network as are relevant to the older person's needs. The caregiver's utilization of these agencies must be planned and organized so that the resources provide a coherent service package. The worker may also be a resource provider, through the worker's own activities and efforts, or may provide resources in a secondary way, through connecting the family with these resources, or through helping to create resources so that they can be available as needed.

There are three categories within the family caregiver modality: education and training, mutual aid, and coordination. The professional roles are generally similar in each of these categories. When focusing on education and training, for example, the worker will often initiate and develop the educational activities through mobilizing community resources. In forming mutual and self-help groups for caregivers, the worker initiates, develops, links, and facilitates the groups, or provides help so that the group can facilitate itself. In coordination of work with family caregivers, the worker will use many of the approaches delineated above. Often the worker will also have to be an intranetwork linker, so that family caregivers' supports and capacities can be aided by the formal systems as these are needed.

IMPLEMENTATION ISSUES

This chapter has presented three varied approaches to supporting the family caregiver. Some implementation issues will be the same for all three approaches; others may be specific to only one or two approaches. Issues specific to a particular approach are noted below.

ADMINISTRATIVE SUPPORT

There is considerable variance among the three intervention approaches in levels of administrative support. Education and training is rated low (L) on the change quotient and low (L) in terms of staff time. This approach has been used by a wide variety of agencies and represents little change, given that many agencies already offer some type of educational program, such as seminars, lectures, conferences, or a speaker series. The staff time required is also minimal as compared to other intervention modalities.

The administrative support required for developing mutual aid/self-help groups for family caregivers is the same as that needed in developing mutual aid self-help groups for the elderly themselves (see Chapter 9). The change quotient is moderate (M), with workers probably requiring additional training in group work as well as community organization techniques. Although the self-help concept is liable to meet with little resistance, some agencies may not feel that work with self-help groups is an appropriate agency function.

The administrative support required for coordination of family caregiving is greater than that required in the above two intervention techniques. The change quotient is rated high (H) to reflect the significant changes required by agencies in adopting this strategy. As can be seen in the program examples above, if these interventions are to be successful, agencies must be flexible. New and different services may have to be created and offered during nontraditional work hours; informal caregivers should be incorporated into the treatment team and, in some cases, paid for the services they deliver. Unorthodox use of staff time and fiscal resources requires significant levels of administrative commitment. The staff time required is moderate (M). A heavier time commitment may be needed in the beginning stages of establishing contracts with the informal helpers than will be needed later on. However, the agency staff must be involved as direct deliverers of service on a continuing basis.

EVALUATIVE INDICATORS

On an effort level, for each of the three invervention strategies, it is important to evaluate and plan for the number and characteristic of the caregivers involved. On an outcome level, the following questions should be addressed for all three strategies: *Was the burden of the family caregivers decreased? If so, in what ways? Was social support of the caregivers in-creased?* For education and training, additional outcomes that need to be measured are the satisfaction of the caregivers with the program and whether there was an increase in knowledge by the caregivers. For mutual aid, agency staff should ascertain the degree of continued participation of caregivers and whether there was an increase in leadership responsibilities exercised by group members. Finally, for the coordination strategy, agency staff will ascertain whether treatment plans for elderly clients were established, and whether there were any benefits to the elderly individuals as a result of services provided by the agency or caregivers.

OBSTACLES AND LIMITATIONS

An obstacle in implementing the education and training strategy is that not all family caregivers will share identical problems and concerns. Therefore, the education and training program must be individualized as much as possible to the needs of the caregivers and their individual pro-blems. One substantial area of difficulty may well be the variation in age and therefore the particular issues and problems with which the family caregivers struggle. Some caregivers have substantially more resources and therefore are more able to be flexible about meeting their own as well as their elderly persons' needs.

With the development of self-help groups, an obstacle may be the lack of supportive services to allow caregivers to attend the program. This may require that the agency offer sitting or transportation services to enable the caregivers' participation. Efforts must be made by the agency to ensure that attending these sessions does not become an additional burden for the caregivers. Some individuals may be reluctant to join self-help groups. Agen-cy staff must recognize differences in class and ethnic background among family caregivers and work through appropriate gatekeepers in the com-munity (such as clergy and physicians) to encourage participation in these groups.

A possible obstacle in the coordination of services strategy is the poten-tial role conflict between caregivers and staff, particularly if one of the members of that informal support system has been designated as a case manager. Danger of rivalry is always great and must be minimized by clear role definition and development of mutual respect through a focus on the goal to be achieved. Redefinition by the staff of their role in this situation as that of service coordinator, not service supplanter, is a vital part of the effort to prevent turf and rivalry problems.

There are also a number of limitations in using any of these three strategies. Two cross-cutting limitations are burnout of caregivers and family rivalries. It is important for agency staff to find and serve caregivers before their burden becomes too great and they reach a burnout stage. Once this happens, the caregiver may wish to leave the caregiving role entirely (perhaps through institutionalizing elderly family members) and may not be amenable to professional efforts to bolster his or her caregiving abilities. Recognizing this, some interventions are aimed at reaching caregivers before they experience too much burden, so they know what to expect and what resources may be available to assist them should any problems subsequently develop. The second limitation refers to tensions between family members involved in caregiving. These family rivalries, of real or imagined causes, may make some caregivers hesitant about seeking assistance.

An additional limitation for the mutual help strategy is that not all people are helpful to one another. Mutual aid operates on the assumption that persons with similar characteristics, conditions, or problems can be supportive of one another. This is not true in all groups and must be monitored carefully. Occasionally, persons with similar characteristics, problems, or conditions may be destructive to one another. Similarity of life experiences is not always helpful unless people have dealt constructively with those life experiences so that they can be facilitative to other people dealing with similar problems.

CAUTIONS

A caution in the use of the education and training strategy is the necessity to recognize the importance of balancing education and training so that emphasis is not just on knowledge but on dealing with feelings and the stresses and strains being experienced. This requires careful planning as to content and variations in style and presentation required for each group session.

An additional caution in the use of the mutual help strategy is that professionals must be careful not to assume leadership roles. Often it is hard for professionals not to step in and take over, particularly if they think the group is floundering. The professional's major focus in working with self-help groups must be to help strengthen the group's own leadership.

Concerning the coordination approach, there is a potential danger in payments to caregivers. The important question is this: Does some aspect of the informal support system become damaged by the payment of money to the caregiver, which, in effect, moves the person into a somewhat more "professional" relationship? This is an open issue to be tested further as experimentation with this approach occurs, but it should be recognized as a caution to consider in applying this modality.

EXERCISES AND STUDY QUESTIONS

1. A church group finds that there are a number of church members who are helping to take care of their aging parents. Many of these caretakers, most of whom are daughters and daughters-in-law of aging parents, are beginning to show signs of exhaustion due to their caretaking responsibilities, especially as their parents become increasingly more feeble. You are a worker in a community agency and are aware that caregiver tensions often precipitate crises that move the older person into institutional care. Your goal is to intervene in order to avoid a family breakdown that might be caused by the burden of this caregiving. Utilizing the family caregiver enhancement intervention, how would you intervene using the education and training modality? the mutual aid/self-help group modality? the coordination and formalization of services modality? What obstacles do you see in utilizing each of these strategies? How can these obstacles be overcome?

2. Which of the three family caretaker enhancement modalities are best suited for your agency?

3. Caregivers need information as well as emotional support. How does your agency address this issue?

SUGGESTED READINGS

Crossman, L., London, C., & Barry, C. (1981). Older women caring for disabled spouses: A model for supportive services. *The Gerontologist, 21,* 465-470.

Mellor, M. J., Rzetelny, H., & Hudis, I. (1981). Self-help groups for caregivers of the aged. In *Strengthening informal supports for the aging: Theory, practice and policy implications.* New York: Natural Supports Program Community Service Society of New York.

Silverman, A. G., Brahce, C. I., & Zelinski, C. (1981). *As parents grow older: A manual for program replication.* Ann Arbor: University of Michigan.

Smyer, M. A. (1982). Supporting the supporters: Working with families of impaired elderly. *Journal of Community Psychology.*

State of Maine, Department of Human Services. (1983, January 31). *Report on the home-based care program.* Unpublished report.

Chapter 6

CASE MANAGEMENT

The third major type of network intervention in our continuum is a treatment approach in which professionals have major involvement. Its aim is to address the issues of fragmentation, lack of accessibility, and lack of accountability in the delivery of services to older persons. Case management is a micro-oriented approach in which the client is an elderly individual. The case manager, a professional agency worker, attempts to coordinate a variety of public and private sservices for the maximum benefit of the client, and in so doing makes the impact of the service both more efficient and more effective.

Traditional case management approaches can be criticized for concentrating on the coordination of professional services to the exclusion of informal support systems. Recently, however, there have been attempts in the aging field to include informal support systems in client assessment and treatment plans. For example, in 1982, as we have noted, the Department of Aging, Commonwealth of Pennsylvania supported research to develop a guide for the utilization and support of informal resources to serve the aging. The department was interested in assisting Area Agencies on Aging to become better informed about the existence and utilization of informal resources for their clients. Recommendations based on this activity include the following:

(1) Service agencies should restructure their philosophy of service to make support and utilization of informal support an important component in meeting the needs of their clients.

(2) Utilization of informal supports should be incorporated into the agency's service management systems.

(3)   Primary caregivers (usually family members) should be included in the assessment process from the beginning to affirm their role in client's care.

(4)   Case managers should assist primary caregivers by providing supportive services and helping to mobilize additional informal supports on the client's behalf (Worts, 1982).

A number of states have already integrated information about informal support systems into client assessment forms. For example, as stated in Chapter 2, the client assessment form utilized by the State of Florida Department of Health and Rehabilitative Services contains a section on services and social support. This chapter will discuss in detail the programs of two additional states, Illinois and Rhode Island.

PROGRAM EXAMPLES

The Department of Aging of the State of Illinois developed The Integration and Coordination of Services for the Health-Impaired Elderly by building on two other programs previously established to meet the needs of high-risk elderly in the community. The statewide Community Care Program provided chore-housekeeping, homemaking, and adult day care. The Information and Referral System (I&R) in Illinois focused on the entry of aged consumers into the service system. Its client-related activities included information, brief assessment, stress and service counseling, referral, follow up, and case finding.

A case management function of the I&R sites was developed in response to a concern for people who remained on the waiting lists for Community Care. The Department of Aging recognized the need for local service networks to ensure access to services and to integrate service plans among providers. With this in mind, the department moved to enhance the I&R system to enable it to assume a visible and central role in integrating services. The stated goal of the new attempt is a systematic approach to ensuring that a client making contact with one service provider in the network had, in effect, contacted the entire network (State of Illinois, 1982).

The I&R sites were funded to address the need for in-home care. Each Community Care service vendor was required to submit, on a regular basis, the names of persons on its waiting list. The I&R staff contacted each person, identified needs, and attempted to arrange alternative services. In many instances these activities led I&R providers to stimulate the development of volunteer and informal resources to meet the needs of clients.

The project report indicates that over 9800 Community Care Program applicants or clients were contacted, and 8400 needs were met in 1982. A typical case example is the following: A participant in an adult day care program was able to avoid hospitalization for a bad foot infection (she was wheelchair bound, deaf, and visually impaired) because I&R staff were able to get a neighbor in the client's highrise to volunteer to provide care for her on weekends.

The 1982 report also indicates that although local I&R networks were requested to become involved in case coordination, this function still exceeded the usual activities of the I&R worker. One of the state's Area Agencies on Aging, however, was described as having progressed further toward organizing a more effective I&R network. In this AAA's area, three providers were given the responsibility of coordinating with other local providers and reporting the activities of all frail, homebound clients in their area. Each of these agencies had the capability of providing case management services. Although a number of difficulties in this attempt were reported, the ultimate goal of I&R services remains to provide every older person entering an institution with an opportunity for a professional review of his or her entire situation to determine if there are means of support (formal and informal) to allow him or her to remain in the community.

Future plans of the Department of Aging and the Area Agencies on Aging in the State of Illinois call for the development of Case Coordination Units (CCUs) in every area of the state, which will be responsible for intake and assessment of older persons' needs and linkage to the appropriate services. Case coordinators will develop individual service plans, utilizing a variety of resources that include agency services and local volunteer groups. Regular follow-up and monitoring are planned, aimed at ensuring that each older person continues to receive services tailored to his or her individual circumstances and needs.

The major objective of the Family and Community Support Systems Model project in Rhode Island was case management "to tailor a plan of care based on the needs of the individual and the families, to meet these needs whenever possible, and to assist older persons in remaining in their home" (State of Rhode Island, 1982). This project of the Department of Elderly Affairs of the State of Rhode Island was a three-year model project funded by the U.S. Administration on Aging. Services were provided to clients based on the results of a functional assessment using a tool developed by Brown University Medical School.

An important element was the lack of an income eligibility criterion for service provision. Services were paid for by third-party reimbursement, client contributions, and AOA grant funds. Grant funds were used to support services and clients that were not third-party reimbursable. This allowed the Health Center, through which services were provided or referred, to include all service components necessary to keep a client at home. Services provided to a client could be determined by the needs indicated in the functional assessment and family care plan, regardless of whether clients or services were third-party reimbursable.

Brown University provided initial and ongoing training in functional assessment. It also analyzed these assessment forms and provided computer-generated individual and aggregate reports. The patient care plan was developed from the functional assessment. Reassessment took place at one- and two-year intervals after the patient's entry into the program. Forms were included that tracked services and staff persons for each client and correlated these with the initial functional assessment. Research questions examined in this project included the relation of patient characteristics to service delivery.

The planners compared the rate of institutionalization of clients of the program with that of Rhode Island's total elderly population. Finding that program's rate to be 1.66%, as compared with the state's rate of institutionalization of 6.88%, the authors concluded that the "program ... did in fact reduce the rate of institutionalization significantly."

The authors identified a number of factors they believed contributed to the program's ability to provide comprehensive, individual care to patients and families. Among these were the flexibility allowed the service providers to pattern case plans based on individual needs rather than reimbursability, given that the grant funded these services. Agency flexibility was noted as an additional critical component. The job responsibilities of the staff involved were determined by the particular needs of clients. Staff often worked "out of classification" when necessary to provide a package of care appropriate to clients and their families. Without this flexibility of the staff, the full benefit of flexible grant funds could not have been realized.

The authors concluded the following:

Flexibility, the assessment and care plan process, the array of services and resources for support services and local ingenuity enabled the Wood River Program to intervene during a crisis and prevent further deterioration. The extremely low rate of institutionalization experienced by the Wood River population is an indication of the effectiveness of this approach. (State of Rhode Island, 1982, p. 12)

The planners thought it was better to develop services that addressed actual needs rather than to tailor program needs to meet service categories and funding criteria. The replication of this program appears to hinge largely on whether funding would be available to allow monies to be allocated for services otherwise not reimbursable to clients whose income eligibility is not established.

SUMMARY: PROGRAM EXAMPLES— CASE MANAGEMENT

— This intervention modality involves the use of professionals to coordinate the informal and formal services used to maintain the elderly person in the community.

— Such approaches typically involve a thorough social support assessment of the client, including information detailing both formal and informal supports available. Interventions aimed at strengthening that support are based on utilizing the assessment information.

— A flexible approach to use of staff time and fiscal resources appears to enhance such efforts. Nontraditional payments, for services not otherwise reimbursable to people who would not meet usual eligibility standards, were found to enhance one program's ability to meet the needs of the clients as determined by the assessment forms.

— As has been noted before, it is clear that such approaches can be sanctioned and encouraged only at high administrative levels and are clearly not within the caseworker's or supervisor's purview to develop without such backing.

PROFESSIONAL ROLES

Case management is increasingly important as a modality because the systems older persons and their families need to use to maintain functioning are complex, fragmented, and uncoordinated. The skills of being able to bring various service providers together so that older persons and their caretakers are able to utilize them consistently and effectively are basic to good professional practice. The role of the professional in identifying the necessary resources and seeing that they work together in a functional way is often the most central service to be offered to the informal systems. The informal system otherwise cannot avail itself of existing help and may thus become overburdened and dysfunctional.

The case management intervention modality calls for the worker to be a coordinator, intranetwork linker, internetwork linker, and manager. The case manager assesses the need, examines the resources currently available in terms of the elderly person's capacities, and the strengths of the support system, and develops a plan for improved and increased utilization of resources. The case manager coordinates the services and resources to provide the maximum cohesion and coherence. The case management modality calls for linkage of various aspects of the informal system and of linkage of the formal network to the informal network. This is one of the major skills a good case manager must have. This modality requires the case manager to be a competent manager so that the services remain responsible to the potentially changing conditions of elderly persons and their informal support systems. The plan will work only if there is ongoing adaptation to the often rapidly changing conditions that are typical of older persons and their informal systems.

IMPLEMENTATION ISSUES

ADMINISTRATIVE SUPPORT

Traditional case management, which involves the coordination and management of *professional* resources for the client, does not represent a significant change from usual agency practices. However, we have defined case management to include also the mobilization and linkage of informal resources for the client. Thus the case manager's role is more complex and represents a higher degree of change than would be required if only formal systems are linked. We have therefore rated the change quotient as moderate (M). Case managers may need additional training in locating and mobilizing family and community resources. There is also liable to be some resistance to this role definition from agencies and staff who may feel that only professional services should be coordinated.

The staff time needed to perform this function has also been rated as moderate (M). For case management to work effectively, as we have defined it, workers need sufficient time to assess completely the current needs and resources of the elderly, including both informal and formal supports. Time must be allocated for case managers to cultivate informal networks in order to tailor a plan of care that builds on the existing resources of the client's networks and strengthens the ability of the client's informal network to provide as much support as possible.

Required professional resources should be used in a way that strengthens, not weakens, the informal network. As we will see later, there are a number of obstacles and limitations in performing these functions that increase the time the worker needs to devote in order to make case management a success. Although case management is less time-consuming than direct clinical intervention with individual clients, it still involves a greater amount of staff time than a number of other interventions.

EVALUATIVE INDICATORS

On an effort level, evaluation should focus on the identification of unmet needs, the number of clients served, and the number of informal and professional resources mobilized on behalf of the client. On an outcome level, several questions should be addressed: *Did intranetwork and internetwork linkages increase? Was there a decrease in fragmentation of services? Were new services created? Did the client's functioning improve?* It should be noted that the first three questions focus on resource systems, whereas the last focuses on changes in individual clients. It is, of course, possible that the overall effectiveness of informal and formal systems can be enhanced without evidence of improved client functioning. In this case, the worker must examine the situations of these clients to see why this has occurred. It may be that the client experienced new problems and needs for which a case management approach is insufficient. If this is true, the worker must reassess the client's current needs and redesign appropriate interventions to meet them.

OBSTACLES AND LIMITATIONS

The appropriate role of informal caregivers may be questioned, and this may become an obstacle to the implementation of this intervention modality. The case manger may be knowledgeable about informal support systems and the advantages of mobilizing these resources on the client's behalf. However, professionals from other agencies may not be as knowledgeable, or they may not believe that informal helpers should be involved in case management and may resist their inclusion. In these situations the case manager may have to provide education and training for agency professionals and/or may need to work individually with agency professionals to help educate them. Negative attitudes may be changed more effectively, however, not through information-giving by the case manager but by other agency professionals seeing the informal helpers in action at case conferences and observing what they have to offer. Another potential obstacle is that in particular agencies case management may involve a redefinition of staff roles from direct treatment to coordination. This change may be resisted by staff.

There are also a number of very real limitations in case management. Our system of professional human services is pluralistic and difficult to coordinate. Everybody wants to coordinate, but no one wants to be coordinated. There are also many gaps in the service system and a lack of services for particular problem areas. It is not possible to coordinate what is not there. On the informal side, as in the clinical treatment modality, clients may resist involvement of their informal network members, or in some cases clients may have a limited or nonexistent network.

CAUTIONS

The temptation for the formal system to exert itself and take over to the detriment of the informal system is always great. Therefore, case managers must recognize this and strive to achieve a true partnership between informal and professional services. (See Chapter 7 for a discussion of how such partnerships were created through the Neighborhood and Family Services Project.) Additionally, case managers must realize that their professional roles are as coordinators, not as direct service practitioners. It is often tempting for workers to intervene directly on behalf of a client when they are having difficulty mobilizing systems to meet the client's needs. To do so, however, weakens the entire case management process.

EXERCISES AND STUDY QUESTIONS

1. A study by a county agency serving older persons shows that clients are using only a small portion of the available community-based services. At the same time, there is a growing demand for institutional services. The study also shows that families and other informal helpers of the elderly find it difficult to gain access to and utilize professional services. These helpers are isolated from other community helpers providing similar services to the elderly. Utilizing the case management intervention, what would you do to address this problem? Where would you begin? Why? What obstacles would you face in such an intervention? How could these obstacles be overcome?

2. Does your agency currently include family, friends, and neighbors as part of the case management plan? If not, what changes would be required for your agency to do this?

3. Can case management address problems of gaps in services and lack of services for clients? If yes, in what ways? If not, what other intervention modalities can be used to address these issues?

SUGGESTED READINGS

State of Illinois, Department on Aging. (1982, September). *Community care.* Annual joint report to the Governor and the Illinois General Assembly on Public Act 81-202.

State of Rhode Island, Department of Elderly Affairs. (1982, December). *Family and community support sytems: Final report.*

Worts, F., & Melton, K. (1982). A guide to the utilization and support of informal resources to serve the aging. Technical Report, North Philadelphia Initiative for Long Term Care. Prepared for the Pennsylvania Department of Aging.

Chapter 7

NEIGHBORHOOD HELPING

Neighborhood helping, as an intervention strategy, involves strengthening the networks of elderly individuals through enhancing their ties with natural helpers and community gatekeepers (pharmacists, physicians, clergy, etc.). This is done in an indentified target area, usually a neighborhood or larger community.

As was shown in the previous chapter, the case management strategy may also involve working with natural helpers and gatekeepers. There are some fundamental differences between neighborhood helping and case management, however. Case management is a treatment intervention focused on individuals in which the case manager works directly with the elderly. Neighborhood helping, on the other hand, is a prevention strategy in which the professional works directly with natural helpers and gatekeepers in order to strengthen the support systems of the entire population of at-risk elderly persons in the community.

Natural helpers are "ordinary" individuals identified by others in the community as being good listeners and helpers. They provide social support consisting of *alleviation of social isolation; emotional support* (encouragement, reassurance) *communication activities* (confidante, listening) and *problem-centered services* (light housekeeping, errands, transportation, cooking) (see Smith, 1975). Advantages of help provided by natural helpers include its easy accessibility, lack of stigma, low cost, mutuality of helping and its basis in proximity, friendship, or long-term acquaintanceship.

A number of authors have developed suggestions and guidelines for working with natural helpers (Collins & Pancoast, 1976; Smith, 1975; Crawford, Smith, & Taylor, 1978). Suggested intervention strategies include consultation and linkage models. The consultation model, developed by Collins and

Pancoast (1976), states that one full-time professional can work with up to 15 natural helpers. The goal is to strengthen natural helpers' abilities to provide assistance to members of their networks and to reach out to other individuals. Professionals can provide natural helpers with information about new programs and services and can also reinforce the work of the natural helpers by assuring them that they are providing a valuable and helpful service. Such a strategy helps the professional as well as the natural helper. Professionals can develop a better understanding of the ways in which elderly in particular communities seek and receive help. The natural helper can offer suggestions, based on his or her extensive experience with elderly in the community, as to how professional interventions can be organized and strengthened.

The linkage approach encourages partnerships between natural helpers and professionals to help identify community strengths, unmet needs, and obstacles to effective service delivery. The premise is that neither natural helpers nor professionals alone have all the expertise and resources needed to solve problems and meet needs. By working together, however, new and innovative approaches to service delivery can be developed.

Informal helpers at the neighborhood level include community gatekeepers—clergy, nurses, pharmacists, physicians, bus drivers, and so on. These individuals are turned to readily because they are available, trusted, or have professional expertise. Numerous interventions have been developed that utilize these resources. In Philadelphia, community gatekeepers were provided training in crisis intervention (Snyder, 1971). In Southern California, rapid transit bus drivers were trained to recognize sensory and motor losses of the elderly. A community mental health center in Spokane, Washington trains a number of service providers, such as taxi drivers, fuel oil dealers, firefighters, postal carriers, and meter readers, to watch for situations and symptoms that may indicate a need for services by the frail elderly (Hooyman, 1983).

Clergy have been singled out specifically as being in a unique position to be effective community gatekeeprs. Haugk (1976) identified a number of characteristics that make clergy especially well positioned to give help to others. They are geographically well located and distributed; they do not charge fees; they have personal relationships with many of their parishioners; they need not wait for people to come and talk with them— they are expected to call on people; there is little stigma attached to talking with a clergyman about personal problems; and they are uniquely positioned for referrals because of their closeness to individuals in need and their professional authority.

PROGRAM EXAMPLES

A number of programs have focused on strengthening the role of clergy in neighborhood helping. The three programs to be discussed in detail in this chapter all include as a goal some aspect of strengthening the role of the clergy in providing help to others.

The first program was directed toward increasing the effectiveness of individual clergy working with the elderly. The program, sponsored by the Louisiana State University School of Social Welfare, Office of Aging Studies, provided gerontological training to clergy. The focus of the training was development of a linkage between organized and informal support systems.

Twelve hours of training were given that were designed to impart a foundation of knowledge of the aging process, to examine the specific needs and contributions of aged individuals, to impart knowledge of community resources available for the aged individuals, and to increase participants' awareness of creative ways to minister to the aged. Examples of training topics include (1) crises often faced by middle-aged people who have aged parents and dependent children, (2) counseling individuals regarding institutionalization, (3) institutionalization, (4) talking with confused senior adults, and (5) fostering intergenerational contact among church members (Office of Aging Studies, 1979, pp. 3-4).

Two training sessions were given to 34 participants, and at least six religious denominations were represented. As part of an evaulation, participants were asked to answer six open-ended questions at the conclusion of the session. A second evaluation focusing on the usefulness and applicability of the content was conducted three weeks after the training. Participants rated the training as helpful and stated they were able to utilize the information gained. Among the recommendations offered by the trainees was the presence of a theologian as trainer when discussing both biblical perspectives and the role of the minister.

The second program, Elderly Outreach, developed by the Catholic Social Services in Albuquerque, New Mexico, also focuses on enhancing the ability of the clergy to provide help to the elderly but in a manner quite different from that of the previous program (Elderly Outreach Program, n.d.). Elderly Outreach is a consultation and coordination service that acts to advise and assist churches in setting up volunteer programs within their own communities. Its goal is for every church to develop a volunteer program to respond to the frail, isolated, and homebound elderly. The program stresses that its function is to promote and assist in the development of volunteer

programs; the administration, leadership, and running of the program always remains in the hands of the individual church. The program is open to any church, regardless of denomination.

As a consultation service, Elderly Outreach undertakes to help a church develop and maintain volunteer programs. Elderly Outreach can help elderly programs (1) define the goals and scope; (2) recruit, develop, supervise, and recognize volunteers; (3) provide opportunities for education through monthly discussion sessions, newsletters, and periodic offerings of specific training sessions in the churches; (4) facilitate communication between churches and agency personnel; and (5) refer elderly with specific needs to appropriate resources. In addition, a central office of the program acts as a clearinghouse for elderly volunteer programs, coordinating their activities and sharing available information. Catholic, Methodist, Episcopal, Baptist, Lutheran, and Presbyterian churches are reported as being serviced by the program, and 43 churches, including about 1000 volunteers, are affiliated in some way with the Elderly Outreach office.

The third program—the Clergy, Agency and Community Case Study/Brown Bag Luncheon—exemplified the linkage approach discussed above in which a partnership between natural helpers and professionals is fostered. It focused on a mix of neighborhood helpers—clergy, agency professionals, and natural helpers from the community. In this program, developed through the University of Southern California/Washington Public Affairs Center's Neighborhood and Family Services Project (Biegel & Naparstek, 1982), natural helpers (many of whom were 60 years and older), clergy, and agency professionals met monthly to discuss problems encountered in group members' caseloads.

Participants were divided into mixed groups of about eight persons each, with each group considering a case written and presented by one of its members. Each case was prepared in advance by the presenter with the assistance of project staff according to a supplied outline. At each luncheon session, after a brief presentation, group discussion ensued. The emphasis of each group's discussion was on seeking alternative ways to address the needs indicated in its case study, to utilize the range of expertise present within the group, to consider workable solutions based on specific case information, and to explore the various resources available for help with the case problem within the community. The monthly seminars were held for several years; attendance was about 25 to 60 persons per session. The feedback of participants after each session was very positive.

The case study luncheons are reported by the authors as having achieved a number of goals. First, through the interaction of community and professional helpers, mutual respect of one another's areas of expertise developed.

There was growing acceptance of the importance of ongoing linkages among all helpers, lay and professional, to meet community needs best. Second, each participant gained knowledge of new or additional resources available to meet these needs. Third, the feedback individual helpers received from their helping peers led to a renewed sense of competence. For example, a young clergyman remarked that in his work he received feedback about the performance of his clerical duties from many sources, except in the area of counseling parishioners. Thus the feedback he received from the case study sessions on his counseling abilities was invaluable to him. Finally, through their review of problematic case examples, the sessions served to indicate areas of unmet need within the community and stimulated the development of new services to meet those needs.

SUMMARY: PROGRAM EXAMPLES— NEIGHBORHOOD HELPING

— This strategy involves strengthening the networks of elderly individuals through enhancing their ties with natural helpers and community gatekeepers in their community.

— Natural helpers are community residents identified by others as being good listeners and helpers. Community gatekeepers include clergy, nurses, pharmacists, physicians, and bus drivers.

— Advantages of using helpers and gatekeepers to provide help to the elderly include easy accessibility, lack of stigma, and low cost.

— A program was described that used a linkage approach to encourage the partnership between natural helpers and professionals. This program was noted as enhancing the mutual respect of the participants, increasing each participant's knowledge of available community resources and sense of competence, indicating areas of unmet need in the community, and stimulating new services to meet these needs.

— A number of programs have been implemented that involve training community people to be more effective in helping elderly residents. Emphasis may be on increasing sensitivity to situations and symptoms that indicate a need for service by the elderly or on increasing their capacity to meet directly the needs of the elderly. An additional program described was a consultation and coordination service that assists churches in developing volunteer programs for the frail elderly in their communities.

PROFESSIONAL ROLES

Neighborhood helping calls for the worker to perform the professional roles of consultant, facilitator, internetwork linker, intranetwork linker, and initiator-developer. It is a modality that focuses on helping a neighborhood to become a strong support system for the people residing there. The effort is to aid neighborhoods to think of themselves as extended families or support systems. The worker is trying to build on what happens more naturally in some neighborhoods by helping other neighborhoods to see the suitability and value of such a function.

Neighborhood helping is a modality that may be utilized when other informal supports are weak or absent. This is especially applicable for neighborhoods with large numbers of older persons who are not receiving needed help. The workers' functions include identification of groups and individuals who have the capacity to provide support, concern, and care for the elderly in the community. Workers serve as consultants to these groups and individuals so that they can perform as service providers. They must facilitate these support systems by providing individuals and groups with resources, the tools of knowledge and skills, tangible supports, and help in assessment and problem-solving as issues arise. The workers' focus is on helping the support system to be strengthened so it can function positively.

The tools for facilitation include an ability to link the formal and informal services in a coherent plan so they can begin to recognize each other as resources. The initiator-developer role is carried out strongly in this modality by identification, recruitment, and support given to the potential helpers so that they can create and expand resources to enhance the capacity of the neighborhood to be a caring system that provides support services to all its residents.

IMPLEMENTATION ISSUES

ADMINISTRATIVE SUPPORT

Neighborhood helping is an intervention modality that represents for many agencies a major change from traditional methods of service delivery. There is strong emphasis on the delivery of services through the informal network and the agency staff developing linkages with such systems. The change quotient has been rated high (H) to reflect both the significant amount

of change required in service delivery methods and to reflect possible staff resistance to such linkage strategies. These issues are addressed more fully under "Obstacles and Limitations."

The staff time necessary to implement this strategy is moderate (M). Neighborhood helping is an intervention modality that usually involves high front-end costs with significant reduction of staff time and significant benefits in the long run. Initially it is time-consuming for staff to become acquainted with neighborhood-based helping networks, to form relationships with natural helpers and gatekeepers, and to develop and implement linkage strategies with these resources. Once developed, the amount of staff time required to maintain these linkages is significantly reduced. Thus the moderate rating is an average rating over time. This may present some problems for workers if agency administrators expect to see quick, measurable results in the short run. Such pressure often forces workers to bypass process to create a visible product. This response to pressure is counterproductive and more costly in the long run than a properly developed neighborhood helping intervention. The agency administrator must understand and support the necessary staff time constraints if this modality is to be successful.

EVALUATIVE INDICATORS

On an effort level, evaluation strategies should focus on the number of informal helpers involved, the demographic and socioeconomic characteristics of the informal helpers, the number of elderly persons who are helped, and the demographic and socioeconomic characteristics of these elderly persons. Outcome level evaluations should address the following questions: *Was there an increase in services provided to the elderly? Were unmet needs of the elderly addressed? Was there an increase in intra- and internetwork linkages?* Again, these questions address both system and individual client issues. Care must be taken to differentiate intervention results on both levels. This intervention modality may be hard to evaluate in the short run. It is relatively easy to evaluate whether linkages occurred; it is hard to evaluate the effects of these linkages on individual elderly clients.

OBSTACLES AND LIMITATIONS

There are a number of obstacles to implementing this strategy. As indicated above, specialized staff skills in identifying, recruiting, and working with natural helpers and community gatekeepers are required. Staff may need specific in-service training and/or consultation to assist them to per-

form these roles adequately. Some informal helpers, such as natural helpers, may be hard to identify. An excellent way to attempt to find natural helpers is to ask clergy, neighborhood leaders, physicians, and human service agency staff to identify them. The following question can be used to elicit this information: "Very often in communities elderly individuals turn to other community residents for help. These residents seem to be effective in helping people even though they have no formal education and training in the helping professions. Do you know anyone like this? Can you give me his or her name?" Once a number of people have been asked this question, it will become evident that some names will be suggested by at least several individuals. These are the natural helpers to focus on. Of course, getting nominations from the elderly themselves is also important.

Agency administrators, as stated above, need to understand the necessity of process in this intervention. One potential difficulty in securing the necessary administrative support relates to accountability and productivity issues. Initial professional activities in this intervention modality resemble community organization rather than clinical activities. Accountability and productivity measures need to reflect this. Realistic ways of accounting for staff time and measuring output may have to be developed.

Finally, attitudinal and value differences between informal and professional helpers may be a major obstacle. Human service professionals often think that they have the major expertise and skill necessary to help people in need, and may believe that community residents can provide little assistance since they are not professionally trained. Community helpers have their biases too. They sometimes think they are the only ones who really care about people and the only ones who really want to help. They may feel that professionals are more interested in their rules and regulations than in helping people. For example, a common statement is that professionals work just nine to five, whereas community helpers are on call all the time.

A limitation of neighborhood helping is the rivalries and turf issues that often arise between professional workers and community gatekeepers. There is, for example, considerable literature on the difficulties mental health and human service professionals and clergy experience when working together (Naparstek, Biegel, & Spiro, 1982). Clergy sometimes feel exploited by agency staff who call on them to provide food, clothing, or shelter for their needy clients but who do not respect their caregiving expertise. Partnerships can be successful only if each party recognizes and accepts the other's expertise. The needs of our clients, as we know, can never be met by the services of professionals alone; therefore, professionals must be sensitive

to and supportive of the appropriate roles that can be played by community gatekeepers.

CAUTIONS

Professional intervention can weaken rather than strengthen informal networks, so care must be taken in the use of this intervention modality. Collins and Pancoast (1976) warn of the dangers of professional consultation with natural helpers that may lead these helpers to feel that they are not qualified to do the helping they have been doing, with the result being a transfer of cases to the professional through the referral process.

An intervention planned with community gatekeepers that ignores the role of informal helpers can unintentionally weaken the overall support system. Several years ago one of the coauthors worked with neighborhood clergy to develop a home care program for the elderly sponsored by a large sectarian agency. The objective of the program was to provide light housekeeping and chore services to the elderly homeowners to help them live independently and reduce the necessity for nursing home care. It was a worthwhile preventive project in which intensive planning was done with clergy and staff of other human service agencies to target services to those most in need and to avoid duplication and overlap of services. Unfortunately, the effort overlooked the informal helpers such as family, friends, and other lay helpers who were already providing many of the same functions the agency workers intended to perform. The result, we found out much later, was that a number of community helpers stopped their efforts, feeling that they were not needed anymore. In actuality, the program soon had a waiting list. If we had recognized the role of the informal helpers, we could have worked closely with these helpers to maximize the number of persons being served.

EXERCISES AND STUDY QUESTIONS

1. Your agency delivers services to elderly persons in an urban, low-income, minority neighborhood. Many residents live by themselves and do not get out often because of concerns of safety and lack of adequate transportation facilities. There are a large number of churches in the neighborhood, some of which offer socialization programs for the elderly. An association of clergy in the area meets regularly to discuss community problems and needs. How would your agency utilize the neighborhood help-

ing intervention to help meet the socialization needs of the isolated elderly in the neighborhood? Who would you involve, and why? What obstacles do you see in utilizing this strategy? How can these obstacles be overcome?

2. Do you think the staff in your agency would be resistant to using this strategy? If yes, why? How can this resistance be overcome?

3. Would this strategy require training or consultation for agency staff? If yes, where would you obtain this needed assistance?

4. What are some of the dangers in utilizing this strategy? How can these dangers be avoided?

SUGGESTED READINGS

Biegel, D., & Naparastek, A. (1982). The neighborhood and family services project: An empowerment model linking clergy, agency professionals and community residents. In A. M. Jeger & R. S. Slotnik (Eds.), *Community mental health and behavioral-ecology.* New York: Plenum.

Collins, A., & Pancoast, D. (1976). *Natural helping networks.* Washington, DC: National Association of Social Workers.

Crawford, L., Smith, P., & Taylor, L. (1978). *It makes good sense: A handbook for working with natural helpers.* Technical report, Portland State University School of Social Work.

Haugk, K. (1976). The unique contributions of churches and clergy to community mental health. *Community Mental Health Journal, 12*(1), 20-28.

Chapter 8

VOLUNTEER LINKING

This intervention involves the creation of ties that are usually targeted directly to individuals in need. Assistance is provided through a helper who is trained, supervised, and organized by a formal agency. Volunteer linking is different from other forms of network intervention. Pancoast and Chapman (1982) studied 30 agencies that operated network intervention programs with various population groups. They stated that volunteer linking

> is the most likely to involve inequality of status between the helper and the recipient—both in terms of socioeconomic status and general coping ability. There is an unequal exchange relationship with the volunteer clearly defined as the helper; while a mutual relationship may be developed and indeed is often encouraged by these agencies, it is not usually part of the standard volunteer role. (Pancoast & Chapman, 1982, p. 223)

Volunteer linking initially demands significant and continual involvement from professionals in the recruitment and training of volunteers and then in ongoing efforts to sustain and enhance the created relationships (Lauffer and Gorodezky, 1977).

There are a number of different types of volunteer programs. In some intervention efforts the primary clients are elderly individuals in need of assistance. In other programs, such as the Retired Senior Volunteer Program, the emphasis is on meeting the needs of older volunteers and matching their interests and skills with an individual in need of service. The third type of program aims at meeting the needs of both groups of elderly persons and involves the recruitment of active, healthy seniors as volunteers for their less well and/or more inactive peers. A fourth type of volunteer effort that has recently gained prominence in a number of areas is intergenerational programming, in which seniors are matched with children or adolescents. Often, the elderly person is the volunteer, aiding the younger individual. There are also efforts in which adolescents volunteer to assist needy seniors.

This chapter describes volunteer programs of three types: programs in which elderly volunteers are the recipients of volunteer assistance, programs in which seniors act as volunteers to other seniors, and intergenerational programs. A separate section on programs in which seniors are the volunteers has not been inlcuded. However, a number of programs using senior volunteers are referred to in all three sections of the program examples.

PROGRAM EXAMPLES

SENIORS AS RECIPIENTS OF VOLUNTEER EFFORTS

There are numerous programs in which seniors are the recipients of volunteer service. One example is a program of the Northwest Salem Community Association in Oregon (Hooyman, 1983). In this program chronically mentally ill older persons without families receive assistance from volunteers of local churches. This linking seeks to create artificial families.

Another program involving volunteers to the elderly is Project Enable of New Orleans, Louisiana, which recruits and trains volunteers from the community who agree to work with an elderly or disabled person in need (Louisiana Center for the Public Interest, 1982). The services the volunteers perform range from grocery shopping and personal care to peer counseling. Project volunteers may be involved in providing personal care to frail elderly clients or reading mail to blind clients. In 1982, Project Enable served 83 clients, all of whom were either isolated, low-income elderly or disabled persons. A corps of 31 volunteers was recruited and trained. Training for volunteers was conducted on five occasions, in addition to community gatherings that brought volunteers and clients together. Recruitment efforts were increased in 1982 when 82 public speaking engagements were made, including radio and talk shows. Three public service announcements were produced for television as well. A training manual was prepared and a trainee's manual was in production.

The authors describe the program as having had a positive and dramatic impact on clients' lives. For example, one client who was found living on tea and crackers and who had not been out of her house for over a year is now eating well and goes out shopping with her volunteer.

The National Consumer League's Medicare Training Project uses volunteers to the elderly in a different way than does the previous program (Personal correspondence, 1983). This project is designed to provide volunteers with factual information and problem-solving skills enabling them to disseminate information about Medicare and Medigap insurance to seniors in their communities. A recent meeting at the Philadelphia headquarters of the Atlantic Richfield Company, whose foundation sponsored the project, involved 38 trainees from a variety of ethnic backgrounds, ranging in age from 23 to 81. Volunteers included a retired physician, a university professor, social workers, hospital employees, and senior citizen center representatives. The trainees found the case studies used in the training useful and thought that the workshop objectives were clearly stated and realistic.

A number of trainees requested even more detailed information, especially about Medicare's billing process, which they perceived as being complex and confusing. Volunteers discovered the elderly had little information about health insurance and desperately wanted reliable data. There was also concern that insurance fraud and abuse are increasing with the elderly as the primary victims. The elderly need accurate information when faced with important decisions about which insurance coverage to buy. The training session was held within the past several months, so evidence of its effectiveness is premature.

SENIOR-TO-SENIOR PROGRAMS

Programs in which seniors act as volunteers to other seniors are much in evidence in the literature. These programs appear to be responsive to the needs of well elderly in providing opportunities for activity, socialization, and use of their skills and to the needs of less well, less active elderly in receiving specific services as well as opportunities for companionship. Unlike mutual aid programs to be described in the next chapter, the relationship between the seniors involved is not reciprocal; one senior is clearly designated the volunteer and the other the client. A number of these programs appear to be effective in strengthening both individual support systems and community networks.

The State of Hawaii reports a number of programs of this type (State of Hawaii, Executive Office on Aging, 1982). One involves respite services in which low-income people aged 55 or over are trained to serve as temporary caregivers for disabled elderly. This is designed to provide nontechnical health care for families providing care for an elderly relative. Another project involves senior companions who are low-income people aged 60 or over. They render supportive person-to-person assistance to frail elderly.

The Trained Listeners Corps (TLC), a project to train volunteer peer counselors for service to the elderly in the community, was developed by Mental Health Services of Southern Oklahoma (1982). The manual includes material on basic communication skills, role transitions, home health care, and transition to institutional care. One day of training is scheduled for each topic. The materials do not indicate where such training programs have been implemented.

An innovative project of the senior-to-senior genre is the Telephone Reassurance Project, cosponsored by Pleasant Valley Manor (a nursing home) and the Monroe County Area Agency on Aging in Pennsylvania, in which nursing home residents staff a telephone network that reaches elderly community residents on a daily basis. The project was developed as an alternative to a telephone network that relied on senior center volunteers. That program was judged to require too much supervisory time and energy. Pleasant Valley's social worker and an AAA staff person determined that recruiting nursing home residents to staff the network could meet social needs for both the callers and their "buddies" and provide a more easily supervised setting for the project.

The project began informally, with the social worker matching nursing home volunteers with community residents needing a daily call. After about six months, the nursing home and the AAA adopted a formal agreement that delineated the roles and responsibilities of each. The AAA conducts the initial interview with clients that includes information that will enable a caseworker to respond to an emergency—name and phone numbers of neighbors or relatives who can check on a client, as well as physician and hospital preferences. The client's name and number are given to the nursing home, enabling the social worker to create a match with a volunteer caller. The social worker also supervises callers and makes sure that they understand their role. Callers telephone the client daily at a prearranged time and contact the AAA if the call is not answered. If this happens, an agency caseworker checks with neighbors or relatives, goes to the person's home to check on him or her, or, if necessary, calls the police to enter the home.

The planners report that all participants have benefited from the program. Clients are provided with additional security and with a friend to help combat social isolation. Nursing home residents are reported to feel useful and to have their self-esteem raised by serving as volunteer callers. Some of the community clients who are not homebound have visited their callers at the nursing home, have taken them out to dinner, and invited them to their homes. Both residents and their buddies have made new friends and broadened their social horizons through the intervention provided by the project.

In Geriatric Outreach for Help (GOH), located in the Fairfax area of Cleveland's East Side, elderly community residents from organized street clubs are trained to provide simple health and social care to all their neighbors 60 years and older, with backup from the seniors' families (A Stronger Project, 1982). This program was designed to combat both minor health problems and social psychological problems such as loneliness, fear, forgetfulness, and depression in a poor black, elderly neighborhood. GOH was planned to be a cost-effective resource leading to less frequent and more appropriate admission to hospitals and nursing homes.

A salient issue was raised by the experience of this project, which produced a morale crisis of the volunteers that was fueled by the agency's top-down administrative structure. A new director improved low volunteer morale by creating what he called a "parallel" volunteer structure, in which the street health worker volunteers are given a feeling of worth by performing administrative functions "all the way up." "In the past, volunteers were often at the behest of the paid people; now it is the staff who serve in a supportive role" (A Stronger Project, 1982). The director indicated that he was convinced that volunteers must be brought into "critical professional operations to ensure the agency's survival in a period of drastic cutbacks." The director's ultimate goal is for the volunteers to manage their own program. GOH has served 697 people and has given its volunteers a feeling of self-worth. Center staff continue to serve training and support functions for the volunteers.

The Volunteer Financial Management System of Corona, California is directed at the specific need of financial management for those seniors who are no longer able to handle their own money matters. Volunteer Substitute Payees (VSP) are senior citizens who are residents of their communities. They are selected by their local senior center and also recommended by other members of the community. They must prove that they have an income exceeding $5000 per year and that they own their own home. These VSPs are trained by the Social Security Administration.

The income of the client is managed by the volunteer, who receives all social security checks and other monies and deposits them in a checking account provided free of charge by a local bank. The volunteer administers the senior's income, pays bills, budgets for extras, or saves money until it is needed.

Safeguards are included to ensure that the client and the VSP are in close contact. In order to protect the client's interest, the volunteers are instructed to confer with the clients on a face-to-face basis twice a month, and to call clients on those weeks when face-to-face contact is not made. VSPs agree in writing to follow the guidelines set down for their services. Failure to follow written procedures and to protect the interests of clients results in termination of services.

The authors have pointed out the uniqueness of this program's administrative framework. It is a cooperative effort uniting city government; the federal government, represented by the Social Security Administration; and the private sector, represented by a local bank. Suggested guidelines for the program clearly spell out the responsibilities of each of these groups. The Senior Citizens Center recruits, screens, and selects the VSPs. The SSA determines a client's need for a VSP, selects one from the list provided from the center and contracts, supervises, and trains the VSP. The SSA also audits all expenditures of clients on an annual basis. The VSP client records are also subject to audit without notice by the senior center.

This Volunteer Financial Management System was designed specifically to supplement services cut by budgetary reductions in the County Adult Protective Services program. The authors report that it has reduced the agency staff's signing of patient's social security checks, and has prevented a number of conservatorships from taking place. It also helps with problems of financial exploitation of senior citizens, as the VSPs are in frequent contact with seniors and their surroundings and usually become friends with their elderly charges.

The Senior Block Information Service is an additional project involving seniors acting as volunteers to other seniors but that has a different emphasis from those programs described above. The Senior Block Information Service (SBIS), part of Services to Seniors of the San Francisco Council of Churches, the contract agency, aims to develop block-based social networks by using senior volunteers to deliver newsletters (Ruffini & Todd, 1979, 1981). In this program, senior volunteers are recruited as block chairpersons to canvas particular blocks, compile a list of people 60 years and over, and distribute newsletters to these seniors on a regular basis. The hope is that in the process of canvassing, volunteers will have conversations with their neighboring seniors. The newsletter is thus used as a mechanism for increasing interaction between elderly volunteers and recipients. The volunteers are viewed by staff as potential leaders of social networks on the blocks and as "middlemen" mediating between the elderly community, the SBIS, and the community of service providers. Volunteers refer any difficult problems they discover to staff.

The authors stress that the Senior Block Information Service is not a model for encouraging the elderly to participate more in self-help activities. Rather, they see it as a low-budget model for encouraging more elderly to participate. They see the fact that volunteers have relatively modest and limited duties that they are able to manage easily as having major importance.

The service is described as a decentralized, flexible program in which volunteers can do as much as they desire and be involved to the extent that they feel comfortable. Although this has a number of advantages, there is also a disadvantage due to the lack of uniformity of service that results. If a particular volunteer does not initiate conversations but merely stuffs the newsletter in the recipient's mailbox, the social support goals of the project are not likely to be fulfilled. As planners see it, the SBIS provides the basis and acts as a catalyst for creation of social networks for those who want them.

INTERGENERATIONAL PROGRAMS

Intergenerational programs that involve linking volunteers of one age group with recipients from another have attracted growing attention in recent years. Foster Grandparent Programs match elderly volunteers with children in need of support and assistance. A similar effort is the Generations Together Program of the University of Pittsburgh (Herron, 1983), which utilizes elderly volunteers in public school classrooms to help teachers with educational tasks and to alter positively children's views of older persons.

In Project YES, the generational crossover occurs in the opposite direction from that of the projects described above. In YES, high school youths are trained and employed to provide in-home support to the frail elderly (Spitler, Wachs, & Kobata, n.d.; Spitler & Kobata, n.d.). YES, a demonstration project under the auspices of the Ethel Percy Andrus Gerontology Center of the University of Southern California, was funded by the Administration on Aging to demonstrate an alternative service model of community-based care for the frail elderly. After the demonstration phase, the project has been continued by the Senior Care Action Network (SCAN), the service coordination agency of Long Beach, California, through local support. At this time, Project YES has successfully recruited, trained, employed, and supervised over 100 high school YES aides who have provided supportive services in the homes of more than 250 frail older people.

Project YES defines the frail elderly as people aged 75 and over who are at risk of being institutionalized due to multiple problems that interfere with their managing the tasks of daily living. As the project planners point out, the needs of the frail elderly often require labor-intensive services that are prohibitively expensive. In addition, staff to provide these services is consistently in short supply, partly because service salaries are generally set at or near the minimum wage, and service positions do not provide the opportunities for career advancement that attract permanent personnel.

Students available for work in their own neighbhoods, therefore, are seen as being potentially critical resources in providing community-based care at an affordable cost. YES addressed the following questions: Can the needs and interests of the frail elderly be matched with the skills and interests of the mature teenager so that each will benefit? How can a positive relationship between the generations be fostered? How can high school youth be prepared to assist the frail elderly?

The planners assumed that five tasks were critical for success, corroborated by three years of operation of the project. These were carefully screening the students, training students for their role, paying aides for their services, providing regular supportive supervision, and maintaining high standards for quality of service.

The project recruited high school juniors and seniors interested in human services and available for part-time employment. Recruitment was carried out with the assistance of the school district. Students recruited were judged as having some degree of maturity, having developed interpersonal skills, and having mastered the academic curriculum. They were seeking employment to help finance their interests and/or their education.

A curriculum was developed and adapted for high school students. Classroom training to prepare them to provide in-home supportive services to the frail elderly was presented. The curriculum was designed to help them achieve the primary goal of providing high-quality supportive services to the frail elderly. The planners thought that the relationship with the clients would be fostered by developing the students' communication skills, helping them to understand the processes of normal aging, and enabling them to gain insights about the world in which their clients lived. The curriculum addressed the skills students had to develop to meet the needs of the elderly clients, and attempted to help students understand that the satisfactory performance of support tasks was the foundation on which a mutually satisfying relationship with the client could be built. The curriculum, presented in its entirety in the project replication manual available from Project YES, was divided into subject units, such as the myths and realities of aging, the processes of normal aging, and communication with the elderly.

The students who successfully completed the initial training and were assigned to serve clients continued to receive two hours of in-service training each week. The in-service training was designed to provide additional information and supportive supervision as the aides worked with their clients. YES aides performed chores such as laundry, dusting, vacuuming, and cleaning the bathroom and kitchen in the homes of the frail elderly. These were the services the older persons needed to maintain themselves in their own homes. They also accompanied their clients on doctor's visits or did shopping for them when necessary. They read to clients and wrote checks and letters for them. Aides also provided respite for family caregivers.

The project stressed that if a task is important to the older person, the YES aide should be a resource to enable the person to complete it. The rationale was that by performing these necessary chores well, the YES aides were also laying a foundation for a personal relationship with their frail elderly clients.

The planning report states that both young and old have gained from the experience of Project YES. YES aides have an opportunity to gain experience in human services, to develop relationship skills, and to develop marketable homemaker skills. Although many of the aides went to college after graduation, those who wished to enter the work world after high school were immediately employed. The older clients received the services they needed to help them remain in their homes. Most of them enjoyed helping the YES aides learn to work and to develop task skills.

Generational Interaction for Today of Oklahoma City indicates the following as its basic purposes: (1) to promote healthy, educated, nuturing, and respectful environments for each generation, and (2) to promote mutually supportive exchanges between generations and the professionals who serve them (Dlugokinski, Olson, Moran, & Rest, 1982; Accounts, 1982). This program originated from the collaboration of a human development specialist, a gerontologist, a school volunteer coordinator, two senior volunteer specialists, a member of a state historical society, and a secretary. They began to discuss collaboration ventures for themselves and the people they served in August 1978. They subsequently created an incorporated, nonprofit organization, G.I.F.T., that issues a quarterly newsletter describing intergenerational projects of many different types. A number of these, discussed below, involve seniors serving as volunteers to younger people.

The principal concepts on which G.I.F.T. is based derive from those inherent in a consideration of social networks and social support: (1) Service of a caring nature cannot be provided by professionals alone; (2) professionals often have poor communication with each other and with the consumers they serve; (3) people of all ages have hidden "gifts" to enhance each other's lives by mutually supportive exchanges; (4) people have the right to receive services based on *need* as well as preexisting pathology; (5) an integration of teaching, service, and research provides for cost-effective and qualitative services; and (6) enriched professionally oriented services are needed in people's daily lives. Mutually beneficial exchange of services, support, and respect are indicated as the critical ingredients and underlying philosophy of all G.I.F.T. endeavors. Barriers to this approach include fragmented planning in human services, transportation, turf boundaries, and legitimation.

A number of G.I.F.T. programs utilize elderly volunteers in unique ways. CARES involved the use of senior citizen volunteers as counselors of adolescent chemical abusers. The volunteers receive both initial and ongoing training. No outcome results are yet reported. Another proposed project involves seniors as foster grandparents in neonatal nurseries of premature and sick infants. These infants are brought to a hospital facility from around the state and are often far from their parents. Other programs reported include an exchange program in which gifts are exchanged between residents of senior centers or nursing homes and children attending day care center or school, and cross-heritage programs in which adolescents receive course credit by developing biographies of neighborhood senior citizens. Senior citizens in this program thus receive a story of their heritage, written and audio versions of their biography, and a sense of their own historical contributions.

SUMMARY: PROGRAM EXAMPLES— VOLUNTEER LINKING

— In this type of intervention, assistance is provided to individuals in need by a helper who is trained, supervised, and organized by a formal agency.

— Seniors may be involved in volunteer programs in the role of provider of help, recipient of help, or as both, as in Senior-to-Senior volunteer efforts. Of special interest recently have been intergenerational programs in which seniors are linked, either as providers or as recipients of help, to young people.

— In addition to traditional kinds of tasks provided by traditional kinds of volunteers, a number of volunteer programs focusing on innovative kinds of help given by unusual helpers are noted. These include programs in which volunteers are trained to disseminate information about Medicare and Medigap insurance to seniors; a telephone reassurance network staffed by nursing home residents; a Volunteer Financial Management System of seniors who manage the financial affairs of other seniors; and a program in which high school students assist elderly community residents.

— The need for careful training and continued supervision, and referral possibilities for volunteers is documented by these projects. This is likely to be especially true for particular groups of volunteers in particular settings, in which the potential for difficulty is clear—that is, teenagers working in homes of frail elderly or seniors working with drug abusers.

— Some of these programs demonstrate that the place of the volunteer in the adminstrative structure of the agency should be clarified. There is evidence that volunteers can often be utilized best, and can experience enhancement of self-esteem, if they are treated as organization staff, not as peripheral "do-gooders." This may necessitate a revised view of volunteers on the part of the agency staff. Reorienting staff toward the function and place of volunteers within the service agency may be required.

PROFESSIONAL ROLES

The volunteer intervention modality uses many types of volunteers to provide a variety of services and support. The professional roles that are relevant to this modality are consultant, facilitator, initiator-developer, manager, and supervisor. The worker identifies the need for volunteers to provide supports to the elderly person and his or her support system. Workers must then recruit, train, supervise, and manage the volunteer program. For this to work effeciently, the worker must provide consultation and supervision to the volunteers.

Workers facilitate the effective use of volunteers by providing help and support to them and by aiding programs to define the appropriate use of volunteers. The need to be clear about the appropriate uses of volunteer services is an important part of the facilitation. Professionals must recognize the importance of providing clear job descriptions, as well as providing training and supervision. These are basic ingredients of success in the utilization of volunteers.

Workers also often have to initiate and develop programs in which volunteers can be used, in both the formal and informal systems. In the course of initiation and development, workers may be able to identify nontraditional uses of volunteers—for example, as quasi-family members.

Workers may also be able to recruit and utilize nontraditional volunteers, such as the persons who are usually viewed as recipients, rather than as givers of services. This notion is an increasingly important aspect of the use of volunteers. It illustrates the importance of recognizing that the helper often gets more help from the experience than does the helped, or at least as much—"the helper therapy principle" (Reissman, 1965). This approach enhances the benefits of the utilization of volunteers to provide services not otherwise available, and enhances the value of mutual help support systems by enabling persons to provide the services they themselves have needed.

The worker is also important in this modality as a manager of the program(s). When volunteer programs are poorly managed, the turnover and retention problems can become overwhelming, often producing failure. Components of success are careful planning and overseeing. Workers need to match volunteers to the tasks to be performed. Once the volunteers are assigned, workers must provide ongoing supervision and guide the problem-solving process as issues arise. These professional efforts often are the difference between effective utilization of this modality and failure. The worker as supervisor is also as vital here as in working with professional staff, and possibly more so. It is possible to misuse volunteers, so that either they or the client may be injured, at worst, and not helped, at best.

IMPLEMENTATION ISSUES

ADMINISTRATIVE SUPPORT

The concept of volunteers is not a new one for most human service agencies. Volunteers are used regularly on boards, in fund raising and public relations, and sometimes in service delivery. The service delivery role of the volunteer is different from other volunteer roles, however, and is one that represents a moderate (M) change quotient. In order to utilize volunteers effectively in service delivery, a significant amount of planning must take place to identify needs that can be met best by volunteers, to recruit and match volunteers, to train and supervise volunteers, and to integrate the volunteers into the agency structure. Incorporation of volunteers into the agency may be resisted by staff who are afraid their jobs might be taken over by volunteers. In fact, given the declining resources for human services over the past several years, this fear may be a real one. Agency staff must be prepared for the use of volunteers and participate in the planning and training as much as possible. Agreement must be reached and communicated clearly about the place of the volunteer within the agency structure so that confusion and hostility do not ensue. Volunteers are part of the staff, but a very particular kind of staff whose place in the organization must be clarified for all parties involved.

The staff time necessary to implement this strategy is moderate (M). At the beginning, it is necessary to plan and organize the volunteer program and its relation to the entire agency. Initially staff time should be spent developing a contract with each volunteer. The contract should include spelling out the ongoing responsibilities of the volunteer and also the ongoing responsibilities of the sponsoring agency or organization. The latter includes training, supervision, interaction with other staff members, and opportunities for personal growth and development. The volunteer must agree to the conditions of the contract in relation to time, hours, frequency, tasks to be performed, confidentiality, ethical behavior, and reporting responsibilities.

Ongoing supervision is vital to the successful operation of volunteer programs. There are several models for providing this supervision: either through the central agency, by the organizational structure within which the volunteer is lodged, or where the volunteer is recruited.

EVALUATIVE INDICATORS

On an effort level, evaluation should focus on the number and characteristics of volunteers (both elderly and nonelderly) and the number and characteristics of service recipients (elderly and nonelderly). On an outcome level, the following questions are important to examine: *Are the volunteers satisfied with their roles, and is this reflected in the retention ratio of volunteers? What services are given by the volunteers, and what needs are addressed by them? Are the elderly clients satisfied with the services of the volunteers? Are elderly volunteers satisfied with their role? Are nonelderly clients satisfied with the services of the volunteers? Can positive changes be seen in the elderly clients which can be attributable to the volunteer program?* In most agencies, this last question must be answered anecdotally because monies are not usually available for a controlled study that compares a randomly selected group of clients who receive a service with another group that does not receive this same service. Nonetheless, one way the agency can learn valuable information about the usefulness of a volunteer program is for both worker and volunteer to keep good notes that can be used to chart client changes and/or reactions to the volunteer service.

OBSTACLES AND LIMITATIONS

There are a number of obstacles to implementing this intervention modality, most of which have been adequately discussed above. To reiterate, this intervention requires careful assessment and planning; it may be threatening to staff; and the required administrative support may be greater than seems immediately evident.

Another obstacle is that it may be difficult to recruit volunteers for service in particular communities, such as those areas perceived to be dangerous, high-crime urban communities. In rural communities, physical distance may present a problem. Volunteers may have to be reimbursed for travel expenses incurred in using their own cars. An alternative strategy in these situations may be volunteer linking by telephone, such as the Telephone Reassurance Program discussed above.

Although, as we have seen, the services provided by volunteers are numerous and varied, a limitation of volunteer linking is that it is not the most appropriate strategy to provide the elderly with health-related services that require specialized skills or long-term commitments. These services are best provided by family members or paid health aides. Another limitation of this strategy is the difficulty in matching volunteers and clients, as not all people are helpful to one another. Great care must be taken in screening volunteers and matching volunteers with service recipients to help ensure appropriate matches, keeping in mind the dual goals of helping both the volunteer and the service recipient.

CAUTIONS

The major caution in using this intervention technique is to recognize that the use of volunteers is no "quick fix" for increasing the service capacity of the agency if fiscal resources remain constant or are reduced. A well-run volunteer program has costs in planning, program development, and ongoing supervision, as we have identified above. Failure to recognize this and to plan properly for a volunteer linkage program may lead to conflicts between regular agency staff and volunteers and to morale problems within the agency.

EXERCISES AND STUDY QUESTIONS

1. Your agency is experiencing a marked shortage of resources for its growing caseload of elderly clients. Because of budgetary problems, the

agency's professional staff cannot be expanded to help meet this increasing need for services. Therefore, you decide to explore the use of volunteers to provide services to part of your caseload. How would you do this? How would you determine what service needs could be met by volunteers? Where would you find volunteers? How would you recruit and train them? Who would supervise the volunteers? How would you decide which clients would receive assistance from a volunteer? How would you match a volunteer with a client in need? How would you integrate volunteers into your program?

2. What is your agency's attitude toward volunteers? What are your clients' attitudes toward volunteers?

3. What "costs" to the agency are there in using volunteers?

4. What "costs" to the agency are there in not using volunteers?

SUGGESTED READINGS

Pancoast, D. L., & Chapman, N. J. (1982). Roles for informal helpers in the delivery of human services. In D. Biegel & A. Naparstek (Eds.), *Community support systems and mental health: Practice, policy and research.* New York: Springer.

Riessman, F. (1965). The "helper therapy" principle. *Social Work, 10*(2), 27-32.

Spitler, B. J. C., Wachs, H. P., & Kobata, F. (n.d.). *Project Y.E.S.: A curriculum guide for high school youth serving the frail elderly.* Los Angeles, CA: Institute for Policy and Program Development, Andrus Gerontology Center, University of Southern California.

Chapter 9

MUTUAL AID/SELF-HELP

This intervention strategy involves the development of ties between elderly individuals. A major aspect of this intervention is the mutuality involved in the helping process. Persons serve both as providers of help to those others with whom they are linked and also as receivers of help from those same individuals. Assistance may be received at the same time by all those involved in a program, as in a support group where the members share experiences and strategies and thereby mutually benefit. Alternatively, members may receive and provide assistance at different times, as in a service exchange program in which an individual provides and receives services of different kinds on different occasions.

This chapter will cover three major types of interventions of a mutual aid/self-help nature: formalized mutual aid/self-help groups, formalized barter or service exchange programs, and programs that create artificial networks among older persons.

The first of these, mutual aid/self-help groups, for the purpose of this discussion is limited to those groups that meet for the goal of mutual support and guidance in response to common problems. These groups typically involve small numbers of persons, mostly non-professionals, who meet on a regular basis for the purpose of sharing accounts of similar personal experiences, discussing coping strategies, engendering mutual support, and identifying and gaining access to community resources (Silverman, 1980). Meetings are typically held on a weekly or monthly basis, and focus on members' discussion of their concerns. Outside professional experts may also be invited periodically to address the group.

Mutual help groups are typically organized around a common concern: a shared illness or condition, or life-cycle transition. Some of the major

advantages of the mutual help group over professional help have been identified as the availability of multifaceted support over an extended period
of time without substantial cost, the sharing of personal experiences that
engender understanding and role modeling, resource sharing, a depth of
feeling that may be unattainable with a professional worker, and decentralized services that are more accessible and reliable than centralized public
services (Haber, 1983).

Abundant literature documents the importance of mutual aid groups for
community mental health (Caplan & Killilea, 1976; Maguire, 1983; PCMH,
1978; Silverman, 1970, 1978). Among the reasons for the effectiveness
of self-help groups, according to Spiegel (1982), are commonality of experience, mutual support, receiving help through giving it, collective
willpower, information sharing, and goal-directed problem-solving. Such
self-help groups can often reach individuals who would never approach professional services for assistance.

The elderly are involved in mutual support groups of many types.
Although the majority of these groups are not specifically limited to membership of senior adults, they are groups in which older persons are likely to
share the predominant concern. For example, numerous self-help groups
for widows have been organized throughout the country with the assistance
of churches, community organizations, and community mental health
centers. These groups provide social support, acceptance, companionship,
and a host of educational and recreational opportunities. Support groups
for people with cancer, heart disease, and other life-threatening illnesses
are also likely to draw elderly members. There appear to be only a limited
number of mutual help groups developed specifically for the elderly. The
two mutual aid programs described in the program example section of this
chapter, however, were developed specifically in response to the perceived needs of elderly individuals and are expected to be composed exclusively of elderly members.

The second type of mutual aid interventions included in this chapter,
the formalized barter or service exchange program, assists individuals to
meet their needs through a formalized exchange of services without the use
of money. In a typical program, individuals register with a central office
those services they can offer to others and those that they need. The central
agency has mechanisms for matching providers and recipients regarding
services to be exchanged and for keeping track of the services given and
received by each of the members.

Such exchange programs offer numerous advantages. They can enhance
the community support systems of participants by stressing the contribu-

tion each individual can make to others. They also provide a framework for socializing with others and for increased community involvement for those interested. In addition, services provided through exchanges are, by their reciprocal nature, more likely to be acceptable to potential recipients sensitive to stigma. Although service exchange programs do not necessarily entail a special concern with the needs of the elderly, those included in this chapter developed out of such concern.

The third strategy of a mutual aid/self-help nature involves programs that create artificial networks among older persons in order to increase the exchange of helping resources. This strategy was identified by Collins and Pancoast (1976) as being used when a natural network is not available or responsive.

PROGRAM EXAMPLES

The examples of the first intervention modality of this chapter, formalized mutual aid/self-help groups, are programs geared specifically for elderly clientele. The first of these, under the auspices of the American Association for the Blind, is a program of materials for the development of self-help peer discussion groups for older persons with sensory loss (American Foundation for the Blind). Funded in part by the Administration on Aging, the program is designed to encourage older people to work together to identify their needs, to learn how to modify their physical and social environment to meet those needs, and to compensate for the loss of one sense through the better use of other senses. The program stresses that anyone interested in sensory problems can participate in and benefit from the "What Are Friends For?" discussion groups and that no prior experience is necessary to lead an effective self-help discussion. The American Association for the Blind offers a basic program package for implementing the groups, which includes information on discussion topics, tips for moderators, and visual materials.

The second program illustrating formalized mutual aid/self-help groups is Senior Actualization and Growth Explorations (SAGE) (see Lieberman & Gourash, 1979). In its developmental stages, SAGE was not a traditional self-help group, as it involved a structured series of activities led primarily by professionals. According to the authors, however, after five years of operation, the program has moved increasingly toward a more traditional self-help organization, in which the elderly take more responsibility for conducting both the governance of the organization and change activities for other aged.

SAGE was developed by a group of lay and professional people who wanted to create a growth setting for older persons, by providing experiential learning designed to maximize their potential. It involves a relatively structured setting in which participants move from one series of activities to another over a nine-month period. The program combines a wide range of what the authors refer to as "change activities" borrowed from diverse sources: group therapy, encounter groups, Zen, biofeedback, meditation, and various physical programs that utilize classical relaxation techniques.

Each SAGE group consists of about 15 elderly people and two to three leaders. Sessions meet weekly for two to four hours. In addition to being guided through exercises that involve the whole group, members are paired to work on interpersonal tasks of sharing and exploration. Informal contacts among group members outside the group meetings are encouraged. According to the authors, within SAGE, while moving from one series of activities to another, friendships are formed, support is given, and relationships are explored. With the spread of SAGE ideology and technology has come the use of the elderly to provide group leadership, as well as the formation of SAGE communities of individuals who have gone through the experience and now have voluntarily developed associations themselves, creating groups that more closely reflect the classic mutual help group modality.

An unusual aspect of this program is the rigorous evaluation study that was an inherent part of the initial project. Such an evaluation was made possible by the unusual circumstances of the program, which included a center in which these activities were offered, and a paid staff supported by an NIMH grant that mandated an evaluation component. For the evaluation, the first 60 people recruited to SAGE were divided into two groups. The first group of 30 were assigned to SAGE groups. The second group of 30 were scheduled to enter SAGE approximately 10 months later, in the interim serving as a control group. Both groups were interviewed before and after the first nine-month session. The same measures were used in the pre- and post-tests.

Subjects' reasons for joining SAGE were to implement personal changes, to begin new activities, and to establish new interpersonal relationships. Many participants wanted assistance in coping with physical, emotional, and marital problems. Others hoped that SAGE would help them overcome negative personal and societal attitudes about growing old. At the end of nine months, SAGE participants found that they had substantially met their initial goals. They also experienced fewer psychiatric symptoms and had a marked increase in self-esteem. However, no consistent evidence of change in health behavior occurred. The group experience appeared to influence the way participants dealt with marital strain but did not have the same impact on strategies for coping with parental role strains, use of the social network, or evaluations of the social surroundings.

The authors admittedly were disappointed in the results of the evaluation, especially the lack of change in health behavior, and indicate further research questions prompted by the evaluation results. They also stress that such an evaluation, involving random assignment to groups and having control group members who wait to participate in the program, becomes neither practically nor ethically viable, once a program is readily available.

The Work Exchange of Milwaukee, Wisconsin (Work Exchange, Inc., 1982) is an example of a successful program, illustrating the second mutual aid strategy covered in this chapter: the formalized barter or service exchange. In this program individuals meet their needs through exchanging skills and services within the community. Trading of services is done through a central banking system, which records service credits debited to the account of the person receiving the service and credited to the account of the service provider.

Work Exchange (WE) was begun in order to help independent older people to continue living on their own for as long as possible. It aims at providing reliable and inexpensive services, as well as socialization opportunities for members. Although membership in the Work Exchange is open to any county resident willing to offer at least one service to another member, its emphasis on serving the elderly is maintained through the stipulation that every service delivery must include at least one person aged 60 years or older as either service recipient or provider.

Currently, WE has over 1000 members, of whom 40% are at least 60 years old. An endless variety of services are exchanged, including snow shoveling, sharing meals, grass cutting, doing laundry, minor appliance repair, lessons in knitting, and service to the program itself or to other agencies. In these exchanges, seniors are both receivers as well as providers of service for each other and for younger individuals. The program's motto is "Everyone has a talent someone else needs."

The Work Exchange indicates the potential for exchange programs to expand into other activities and services that strengthen community support systems. The group puts out a newsletter that serves as an effective community resource. Members submit articles, poems, recipes, special services offered or requested, and so on. The newsletter also lists members' birthdays and announcements of community events and describes exchanges that occurred: "Cecil, aged 67, repaired a leaky faucet for a very satisfied Lela (aged 67). The job took him one hour to complete." The Work Exchange also sponsors support groups, which meet once or twice monthly on a neighborhood basis. These groups, led by facilitators, include discussions and guest speakers. Work Exchange members receive credit for attendance at meetings that can be used toward exchanges.

Additional service exchange programs, which operate similarly to the service exchange aspect of Work Exchange, include the Barter Network of Marin County, California with approximately 300 members, and the exchange bank component of Project LINC, a three-year demonstration project of the Andrus Gerontology Center of the University of Southern California.

A program that demonstrated a number of the difficulties involved in developing and sustaining a service exchange program for seniors was the Senior Citizens Service Exchange Program, a research and demonstration project of the University of Pittsburgh School of Social Work in cooperation with The Center, a multiservice senior center in Sharpsburg, Pennsylvania (Shore, Yamatani, & Gordon, 1982). This effort was funded by the Commonwealth of Pennsylvania Department of Aging for a five-month period. The program aimed at establishing a service exchange program at three senior centers in Allegheny County. Mechanisms were set up for registering members, who indicated the services they wished to receive and those they could provide to others, and for a system of credits by which the contributions and deductions of each member were recorded.

The congregate feeding program at each center was asked to participate in this program, and recruitment attempts were limited to this population. The project planners found that recruitment involved a long process of introducing the idea of an exchange program, letting people get used to the idea, and then gently encouraging their involvement. It was found that from 20% to 25% of lunch program participants eventually registered for the program.

A variety of services, such as baking, mending, gardening, window washing, and painting, were offered or requested at the centers. A number of valuable exchanges took place. The project staff sensed, however, a reluctance on the part of a number of seniors to request help. "I can manage on my own," was a common response of seniors to the program. One of the final recommendations of the project was for additional recruitment efforts with a wider population base who might be better able to fill some of the requests for very specific services, such as grass cutting, to a greater degree than a membership composed solely of seniors. It was also recognized that successful recruitment would be better achieved through a continual effort implemented for a period longer than the five months alloted by the project. Nevertheless, a number of useful services, such as household repairs, were exchanged in this short time, with great satisfaction express-ed by both recipients and givers.

The Neighborhood Network of Riverdale, New York is a program in-volving the exchange of services with a somewhat different emphasis than the programs discussed above. The Neighborhood Network involves swap-ping services at the community level and, in addition to individuals, also involves agencies as trading partners (Noberini & Berman, 1983).

The network developed out of the Community Advisory Board of the Hebrew Home for the Aged at Riverdale. The board, including represen-tatives of 20 major community institutions and key political figures, was established to develop an ongoing dialogue between the institution and the surrounding community. The goals of the network are (1) to provide a climate conducive to the creation of cost-effective and efficient delivery of services to the aged in the Riverdale community and (2) to develop a model for neighborhood collaboration as a prototype for other communities.

Community outreach was established as a priority in implementing such a model. A conference was held to bring together professionals who worked with or on behalf of the elderly, professionals who were concerned with issues of aging and aging populations, and local senior citizens. In the three months preceding the conference, the coordinator met individually with the administrator or president of each major community organization in River-dale to explain the neighborhood network concept and its possible advan-tages, and to enlist support in terms of delegates to the conference.

Two hundred delegates attended the conference. Of these, half were pro-fessionals representing 50 agencies and half were senior citizens. The con-ference conducted workshops on various subjects, such as older persons and their families, and senior health needs and information. Delegates were asked to fill out a swap sheet indicating their needs and the resources they could offer and also a sheet to indicate their interest in a formal exchange agency. Of the participants, 75% returned swap sheets and 60% indicated an interest in a formal exchange organization. An evaluation of the con-ference was conducted through the use of an evaluation form filled out by the participants. Over half of the participants completed the evaluation, with the majority rating the conference as excellent, and the rest as good.

A final outcome of the conference was a needs and services "Yellow Pages." In this publication, each agency lists its needs and skills, space, and/or equipment it can share. This is designed to permit agencies to initiate swaps directly with each other, without the need for a brokerage organization.

This project reports a number of innovative barter programs implemented by community agencies as a result of the conference. College students studying foreign languages are matched with residents of a home for the aged who speak this language. The student gains an opportunity to improve language skills and to learn about the country's lifestyle and customs. The older person is placed in the prestigious position of teaching and sharing. In "Growing Together," fifth-grade schoolchildren visit weekly with a group of elderly residents in an apartment complex under the auspices of a long-term care institutions. In exchange, this institution offers the children a six-session minicourse on the problems and concerns of institutional living.

A third project involves the services of elderly volunteers to stuff envelopes at a nutrition center and to organize large bulk mailings by zip code at a cultural center. These clerical services are traded for free concerts presented at the nutrition center. This swap of services diminished the clerical costs of one agency and provided meaningful work and cultural pleasure for the members of the other. This type of barter system involves a variety of community agencies to a much greater degree than those reported above, and suggests areas of expansion that these established senior service exchanges could adopt.

The paper reporting this project outlines a number of observations and recommendations that the authors state may be especially useful to individuals or communities interested in developing urban neighborhood networks. They suggest, for example, that the most important single factor in motivating the development of barter arrangements is the sense of frustration and pessimism that results because of the inadequacy of traditional sources of support. They add that more and more human service workers have discovered that to rely on one agency to provide all necessary services is financially irresponsible and that interagency rivalry is destructive. They indicate that the task of neighborhood network organizers is actively to point out the merits of cooperation and exchange as an alternative. The most striking observation that resulted from experiences with the neighborhood network was the enormous enthusiasm with which the idea of network of exchange or barter was greeted by both the aged and their service providers. They report that both groups of people clearly identified themselves as victims of current social changes and welcomed with relief the opportunity to take positive action to ameliorate the problem.

A program using the third intervention modality presented in this chapter, creating artificial networks, is The Elder Program of the University of

Louisville Gerontology Center, Louisville, Kentucky (Crowe, Ferguson, Kantrowitz, & Biddle, 1981). The Elder Program, supported through a three-year Administration on Aging Model Project grant, was aimed at preventing dysfunction of older participants and their neighbors and friends by developing a concerned group of persons in the neighborhood who had the needed skills and information to help those coping with problems. The underlying philosophy emphasized self-help, stressing that older adults have both needs and resources and are both potential receivers and providers of service. The Elder Program was an educational program that emphasized information, resources, and skill development. A workbook for participants was developed at the fifth- to seventh-grade reading level in large print, which included information on methods of outreach to others, individual helping and problem-solving, and daily living needs such as health and finances. Eleven groups with over 200 participants were formed in six neighborhoods of different types. A recruiter was hired who was over 60 years old and a resident of the area.

Eight weekly meetings utilizing workbooks, films, and guest speakers were held. Sessions involved discussions, exercises, and task assignments. Evaluation instruments were administered at the beginning of the educational program and at two- and six-month intervals after its conclusion. The 11 groups were all found to have continued beyond the eight weeks, and findings indicate a significant increase in the amount of helping activities occurring between group members. In addition, some of the groups also had reached out to others in the community.

SUMMARY: PROGRAM EXAMPLES—
MUTUAL AID/SELF-HELP

— Three major types of mutual aid/self-help intervention models are presented: formal self-help groups that meet for mutual support and guidance, formalized barter or service exchange programs, and programs that create artificial networks among older persons to increase the exchange of helping resources.

— Interventions of this type tend to embrace an underlying philosopohy that sees the individual as both a potential recipient and deliverer of service. The assumption is that at different times and under different circumstances, the elderly individual will both provide help to others in the program and accept help from other members.

— A number of these programs, especially of the service exchange type, are cross-generational, with members of different ages providing services to one another. Mechanisms can be included that ensure that the focus remains on serving seniors in these exchanges.

— A number of these programs have also been seen to reach out beyond exchanges on an individual level to those on the community level, which includes agencies, or groups of individuals giving and receiving services to other agencies or groups.

— The service exchange programs that have been successful have a strong central organization that works to recruit members, develop a mechanisms by which exchanges can take place, and take charge of the bookkeeping of credits and debits that is involved in exchanges. Especially as groups grow larger (and some are noted to have over 1000 members), a strong central organizing and coordinating agency is likely to be a necessary part of exchange networks.

PROFESSIONAL ROLES

The mutual aid/self-help model is a modality that builds on the strengths of shared experience, problems, or characteristics. The emphases in the professional roles that are vital to the effective application of this modality are on the recognition that people who share a common characteristic, problem, or condition have strengths that, when expressed, are enhancing for them and for their support systems. The professional worker who wishes to use this modality must perform the roles of advocate, consultant, facilitator, initiator-developer, and resource provider. The advocacy herein is related to the need to promote groups, supports, and service exchanges on behalf of clients and their support system. This often means having to create the mechanisms through which people can receive help, such as mutual help groups of varying types or service exchange programs. It also means advocating for people to be able to use and share their experience as a way of focusing on their strengths rather than their weaknesses. This is a vital principle that often is not fully realized or acted on by professional workers.

The important consideration here relates to both "case" advocacy and "class" advocacy. Case advocacy is the activity of seeking resources, including power, knowledge, and control for an individual client or client group. Class advocacy is pressing for systems change in order to achieve the goals of bringing more power, knowledge, and control to entire segments of society. In each the effort is to provide an environment for strengthening capacities to cope and manage through the sharing of mutual experiences and capacities.

In using mutual aid/self-help as a modality for intervention with older persons and their support systems, workers must advocate for adequate opportunities for people to come together on their own behalf. The worker becomes a cnsultant to the group and to individuals in the group. To carry out this role, workers must recognize that it is not appropriate to be the director, controller, or provider. The worker's role is to strengthen the group's capacities to provide resources and mutual suppport.

Workers also initiate and develop the opportunities for mutual aid and facilitate the mutual aid process by providing support, information, and, above all, positive regard for the capacities of the individuals and groups to perform. The worker also provides necessary resources such as meeting space, clerical and office help, transportation, and money for mailings.

Although the above roles may not appear difficult to play, it is often difficult for the worker not to move in and assume leadership, especially if the group is floundering. In fact, individuals in the groups sometimes expect the worker to take over. This may put the worker in a double bind situation: If the worker does indeed try to take over, the group may then react with hostility.

It is important for workers utilizing this modality always to be aware that some persons are destructive to others in the group. Workers must monitor the process sufficiently so that people who have used their life experiences negatively do not damage other individuals in the group or destroy the group's effectiveness. Some moderating of individual and group interaction is often necessary, including, at the extreme, separation of some persons from the group.

IMPLEMENTATION ISSUES

ADMINISTRATIVE SUPPORT

The program examples focused on three somewhat different mutual aid strategies: mutual aid/self-help groups, barter-service exchange programs, and programs that create artificial networks among older people. Overall, we have rated the change quotient as moderate (M), although there is some variance among the three techniques of this intervention modality. There has been tremendous growth in the number of self-help groups over the past decade; for many human service workers this is not a new concept.

Nevertheless, if an agency has not previously used self-help groups as an intervention strategy, a moderate amount of change may be required. Workers will probably need additional training in group work as well as in community organization techniques. Although the self-help concept is liable to meet with little resistance, some agencies may not see that work with self-help groups is an appropriate agency function. Barter or service exchange organizations, on the other hand, are not a widespread phenomenon. Agency administrators and staff must be educated as to the role and function of these organizations and as to what role, if any, their agency can play in stimulating the development and nurturance of these groups. The creation of artificial networks for the elderly involves the highest degree of agency change. Staff should receive training to utilize this technique because community organization skills are necessary to develop these networks.

Overall, we have rated the staff time to implement the mutual aid/self-help intervention modality as low (L). For the self-help groups and service exchange strategies, the ongoing staff time needed is low because the worker's aim is to help these types of groups become as independent as possible. Although a higher amount of staff time will be needed in the initial phases, in the long term this commitment should be quite low. However, with the strategy of creating artificial networks, the required staff time will be greater. This is a product, as in the neighborhood helping modality, of the time it takes to become familiar with a community, its leadership, and helpers to develop interventions through the existing helping networks. This strategy also takes a larger degree of community organization skills than do self-help or barter group strategies, which have greater individual and group work components.

EVALUATIVE INDICATORS

On an effort level, evaluation should focus on the number and characteristics of participants (elderly and/or informal helpers). On an outcome level, the following questions should be addressed: *What is the retention rate of group members? Is there an increase of leadership responsibilities exercised by group members? Is there a reduction of stress and loneliness of group members? Is there a increase in social support of group members? What are the amount and types of service exchanges? Is there an increase in functioning levels of elderly assisted through service exchanges? Is there an increase in functioning level of elderly assisted through the creation of artificial networks?*

OBSTACLES AND LIMITATIONS

An obstacle to the development of mutual aid/self-help groups and programs is the reluctance of some elderly individuals, for reasons of pride and privacy, to join them. Typically, for example, ethnic working-class elderly are underrepresented in self-help groups for widows. A possible strategy to overcome this resistance is for agency staff to work with clergy and other community leaders and enlist their support in contacting potential participants and in endorsing and recommending the program to them.

Particular individuals also may be reluctant to join a service exchange program. Workers must realize that depending on the community, some elderly individuals may not want to use this service because they define themselves as only needing help and not as capable of giving help or vice versa. For a number of elderly, asking for help carries a stigma that may make them unwilling to participate in this type of program. The worker should help these individuals become aware of their own strengths and resources. Often elderly persons do not realize how much they really have to give to others. Sometimes these issues can be dealt with more effectively by informal helpers and leaders rather than by agency workers. Thus before beginning to recruit elderly for a service exchange program, the worker should develop a "feel" for what the community reaction might be and how best to implement the program in light of anticipated reactions.

There are a number of limitations in using the mutual aid/self-help strategy. One limitation, which we have already seen with other intervention strategies, is that not all persons are able to be helpful to others with similar conditions, characteristics, or problems. Some screening or careful facilitating has to occur to avoid behavior in the group that may be destructive to some group members or that may precipitate their departure or withdrawal from the group. The issue of how active the professional should be with the mutual aid group is an ongoing issue that has to be dealt with not only in terms of definitions of the relationships between the professionals and the self-help group members, but also at different stages of the group as the group's needs shift and change. Another potential limitation in the use of mutual aid is that the needs of all persons in the group are not identical. There should be an opportunity for either individualization or for determining that alternative resources may be more suitable for some persons. It is not a failure of a group when members decide to withdraw, if the basis for the withdrawal is their own readiness to move on to another phase of their lives. In fact, groups vary widely in the length of time members remain in the group.

CAUTIONS

An important caution in the use of any program strategy in this intervention modality is that care must be taken that professionals do not assume leadership roles. This is particularly crucial in the development of mutual aid/self-help groups. Professionals can supply specific practical help to self-help groups without sapping the groups' autonomy. For example, as stated above, professionals can provide a meeting place; minimal funds for telephone; mailings, refreshments, and the like; information relating to welfare, housing, medical or legal information; referrals; and social and emotional support.

EXERCISES AND STUDY QUESTIONS

1. An agency serving the rural elderly is faced with the problem of fairly isolated older persons living in the same communities who do not know one another. Many of these persons can still manage the activities of daily living but are experiencing some sense of isolation and concern about their safety. They are unsure if they will be able to maintain themselves in their own homes and are worried about their futures. You see the possibility of helping many of these persons to find and help support one another, both tangibly and emotionally. Using the mutual aid/self-help intervention, what would you do to address this problem? How would you bring these individuals together? What resistances would you anticipate? How would you address this? What professional roles would workers utilize?

2. Which mutual aid/self-help support strategies are most appropriate for your agency to use: mutual aid/self-help groups, barter-service exchange programs, or creating artificial networks? What are the advantages and disadvantages of each for your agency?

SUGGESTED READINGS

Caplan, G., & Killilea, M. (1976). *Support systems and mutual help.* New York: Grune and Stratton.

Lieberman, M. A., & Gourash, N. (1979). Effects of change groups on the elderly. In M. A. Lieberman, L. A. Borman, & Associates (Eds.), *Self-help groups for coping with crisis.* San Francisco: Jossey-Bass.

Noberini, M. R., & Berman, R. U. (1983) Barter to beat inflation: Developing a neighborhood network for swapping services on behalf of the aged. *The Gerontologist, 23,* 467-478.

Silverman, P. R. (1970). The widow as a caregiver in a program of preventive intervention with other widows. *Mental Hygiene, 54,* 504-547.

Chapter 10

COMMUNITY EMPOWERMENT

The concept of community empowerment is central to the development of intervention models that build on community strengths to overcome identified obstacles to service delivery. Our definition of community empowerment is dependent on the concepts of *capacity* and *equity* (Naparstek, Biegel, & Spiro, 1982).

Capacity has three components. It is an individual's or group's ability to (a) utilize power to solve problems, (b) gain access to institutions or organizations that serve them, and (c) provide nurturance to others. Power and nurturance are seen to depend on different types of resources. Skills and financial resources are necessary for power. The skills required for effective use of power include organization, leadership, management, and the technical expertise to plan, conduct research, and implement programs. The defining elements of the nurturance dimension are human and community resources. Included here are people interacting and providing social support to one another on both individual (family, friends, neighbors) and organizational levels (churches, ethnic clubs, self-help groups,). *Equity* is based on whether individuals or groups define their investment as equal to their return and whether they see themselves as getting their fair share of resources as compared to others (Naparstek et al., 1982). Intervention programs utilizing this modality aim at increasing the capacity and equity of elderly persons. Empowerment programs build on community strengths to identify service needs and to work toward mobilizing the necessary resources — political, economic, and attitudinal — to meet these needs. The individuals involved come to see their own unique qualifications to define those needs not being met in their communities and to shape services responsive to those needs.

A number of projects that have used empowerment strategies have been noted earlier as arising from self-help groups of caregivers to the elderly. A self-help group of wives of disabled men, Women Who Care, was discussed above as applying for and receiving funds to start a two-year project for respite services, once the need for such services became clear to them. The Community Service Society reports that it facilitated the Caregivers Network, a consumer advocacy group active in presenting testimony at public hearings, sensitizing legislators, professionals, and the media to their role, and identifying unmet needs. As members of a group under the auspices of the planning department of the Philadelphia Area Agency on Aging, 35 seniors from centers in the area work for legal changes on pertinent issues. Among other activities, the group is involved in mass writing efforts and disseminating information to other seniors. Phylis Ehrlich developed a project called the "Mutual Help Model" that utilizes networking methods to create neighborhood groups that are organized to help with any problems that arise regarding aging services (Worts & Melton, 1982). Three additional community empowerment projects involving the elderly will be described in detail below.

PROGRAM EXAMPLES

In New York City, the Citizens Committee for New York City, Inc. sponsors a program called the Mutual Aid Project (MAP). The goal is to help older people in neighborhoods provide services for themselves. Staff organizers are available to local groups and provide advice, technical support, and organizational assistance. The residents themselves decide what projects are needed; the staff functions only in a supportive role to help the residents develop projects they themselves have identified. MAP publishes a handbook that discusses projects organized by member groups. Examples include self-help projects, projects for the homebound, consumer education projects, urban gardening, and cooperative and exchange projects.

The Neighborhood and Family Services Project of the University of Southern California/Washington Public Affairs Center developed a model that builds on the unique strengths and resources of communities and uses these strengths to identify and alleviate obstacles that prevent community residents from seeking and receiving help. Instituting the Community Mental Health Empowerment Model in a number of communities involved meeting a number of objectives (Naparstek et al., 1982).

(1) Creating awareness of the neighborhood's strengths and needs on the part of its residents. In this stage community residents were involved in gathering data on help-giving and help-receiving in the neighborhood. Both objective statistical figures and subjective interviews with community leaders and helpers were included in this process. Also, an inventory was made of all local human service agencies.

(2) Strengthening the neighborhood lay helping network. The objective was to strengthen this network and to help residents acquire confidence in their abilities to deal with mental health issues as nonprofessionals so that they would be able to interact with professionals as partners. The process involved collecting data, analyzing it, and setting priorities for intervention by the community. Working committees were then set up to develop demonstration programs such as self-help groups, family communications seminars, and crisis hotlines.

(3) Strengthening the professional helping network. The fragmented and uncoordinated professional helping system was strengthened by bringing together professionals who worked in the same geographic area yet were rarely in contact with one another.

(4) Forming linkages between the lay and professional helping networks. Once the previous objectives had been achieved, the lay and professional systems were ready to develop a partnership, fully aware of their differing roles and agendas.

(5) Linking the lay and professional helping networks and the macrosystem. Once the neighborhood empowerment process was on its way, the community had to examine the larger forces that affected it. Information was gathered on state and local mental health and human service plans. Local sources of funding were scouted, and linkages were established with local funding institutions and organizations. The authors stress the importance of this stage especially if the accomplishments of this process are to be long-lasting.

Through this model linkages were developed between community and professional helping networks in a number of communities. Professionals acted in an advisory capacity to community groups, rather than the more usual process of community residents being advisors to professionals and their agendas. Community residents increased their abilities to develop programs to meet needs they themselves had identified. Programs specific to the elderly that were eventually developed by this project included a 60-page directory of services for the elderly, self-help groups for widowed individuals, a hotline staffed predominantly by elderly volunteers, and an elderly advocacy group. Many of these projects continued after the initial four-year federal funding ended.

Whereas the above two examples utilize the development of needed service programs as part of the empowerment strategy, the focus of the group called the Grey Panthers is solely on social change through social action. The long-range goal of this organization is making society more just and humane and the "liberation and empowerment of all persons who are oppressed and powerless — among them non-white people, women and the aged" (Kuhn, 1978, p. 360). Objectives include fighting agism and discrimination based on age, developing and building power through coalitions for political and social action, and humanizing society.

The Grey Panthers are a Philadelphia-based organization founded in 1971 by Maggie Kuhn. They have been involved in a broad range of social action issues in Philadelphia, Chicago, Boston, and other cities. In the mid-1970s they organized a coalition of groups of older people in Philadelphia to focus on mass transit problems. They wanted reduced fares for individuals 65 years and older and rescheduled bus routes. The coalition conducted research on declining ridership and increased fares and costs in Philadelphia. Innovative programs in other cities were examined. A meeting of the Transit Authority Board was held, and older persons turned out in large numbers. They argued their position based on facts and research. Their homework and display of force won the day, and the Transit Authority agreed to their demands. Kuhn reports that ridership increased the following year.

In Chicago the target was the American Medical Association, and the tactics were even more direct: mass action picketing. The Grey Panthers wanted the American Medical Association to help improve the health system for the elderly by lobbying HEW for changes in Medicare regulations on home care, by urging that mandatory gerontology courses in medical schools be required, and by appointing a consumer representative to the AMA House of Delegates.

SUMMARY: PROGRAM EXAMPLES — COMMUNITY EMPOWERMENT

— This intervention strategy is aimed at increasing the capacity of older persons to use power to solve problems affecting them and to increase their ability to gain access to institutions and organizations that serve them.

— Efforts have begun to increase this capacity that involve linkages between formal services and older persons in their community. The formal agency provides a framework in which community residents can receive training, guidance, technical support, encouragement, and other assistance that enables them to develop their own programs to meet needs they themselves have identified.

— A number of advocacy groups are noted as having evolved out of groups with other agendas when needs are identified and solutions to these needs are sought by the older person and their social support systems, in the absence of existing services.

— Some efforts involve the joint development of service programs and advocacy; others are limited to advocacy and social action only.

PROFESSIONAL ROLES

Professional roles utilized in the community empowerment modality include those of advocate, consultant, facilitator, internetwork linker, intranetwork linker, and initiator-developer. Workers advocate for the community's right to declare its own needs and to seek the resources to meet these needs. Workers also advocate on behalf of the community so that it can accomplish its goals.

In addition, workers must serve as consultants to the community in helping it both to define its needs and its goals and in its efforts to plan its strategies to achieve these goals. Workers must be aware of when it is appropriate to do the advocating and when it is appropriate to be a consultant, helping the group do its own advocacy. Clearly, with older persons, as with younger persons, the desired goal is to help people to help themselves. An assessment is always necessary to determine the degree of capacity of clients to achieve their goals. With older persons, careful and repeated assessments are necessary to avoid unnecessary debilitation because of insufficient or delayed responses to their needs. On the other hand, often there is an assumption about older persons' incapacities to function on their own behalf, and therefore a substantial tendency for professionals, as well as families and other caregiving persons, to take over the control and not give the older person the opportunity for the mastery of accomplishment on their own behalf.

Being facilitative essentially means that the worker is helping others, including other persons and their support systems, to do the doing by increasing their capacities for problem-solving. The facilitator must always try to provide the support, help, and resources to assist older persons meet their own needs more effectively and to help others to become more active on behalf of older persons.

The linker role is basic to the community empowerment modality. The linkage in using this modality is both between the formal and the informal systems. The worker attempts to build the infrastructure of the community so that the community will be strengthened and can provide more adequate supports and services to its residents, especially its older residents. The strengthening includes building stronger ties between the informal and formal systems in such a way that the informal systems are recognized for their importance and are aided, not taken over, by the formal system. The approach also includes helping informal systems to find and give support to one another.

The initiator-developer role assists the community to organize and be effective in seeking and getting what it needs to meet its goals. The worker with a focus on the elderly is especially crucial in this modality, because the elderly residents are often relatively invisible, and therefore their needs are not considered within a community as it identifies its problems and strategies. Often older persons are undervalued or devalued, so that their contributions to the life and organization of a community are not recognized. Furthermore, their needs may not become a high agenda item in a community, unless they can either advocate effectively for their needs or enlist a strong advocate.

Workers using the community empowerment strategy can assist in building bridges across groups divided by age, race, social class, or gender that do not perceive their common interests because of these divisions. Workers can be enormously helpful, not only to older persons but also the entire community, which is strenghtened and empowered by its recognition of the common interests and needs of all its citizens. Communities can be helped to reduce destructive conflict between groups by advocating for the recognition of the commonality of the concerns and interests of all residents.

IMPLEMENTATION ISSUES

ADMINISTRATIVE SUPPORT

In order for community empowerment strategies to be implemented successfully, a high level of administrative support is required. This modality requires the highest level of administrative support of any intervention strategy in our typology. The change quotient is rated high (H), to reflect both the significant amount of change this modality may represent for the agency and because of expected high levels of resistance that may come from both staff and community. This intervention is very different from usual agency service delivery strategies because it is an organizational technique used to build control and power for community residents. Also, at times this approach involves planned conflict as an intervention tactic. Highly specialized staff skills are required, and staff will need considerable training to carry out this technique effectively.

The staff time has been rated high (H) to reflect both the time needed for staff training and because of the heavy investment of time required to get to know the community and its leadership in order to build a grassroots organization and to help that organization develop strength and independence. Although large amounts of staff time will not have to be provided on an ongoing basis, the staff time required in the short run will be considerably higher than in the neighborhood helping modality. In fact, the so-called short run is also likely to be longer. If this strategy can be implemented successfully, however, the initial investment of staff time will have a large payoff. For example, as indicated in the program examples above, program components of the Neighborhood and Family Services Project have continued several years after the end of the initial federal funding.

EVALUATIVE INDICATORS

On an effort level, evaluation activities should examine the number and characteristics of participants. On an outcome level, the following questions are important to focus on: *What issues were addressed? What changes occurred in the informal and formal systems? Was there an increase in intra- and intersystem linkages? Were new services developed? Was there an increase in the capacity of the community to address unmet human needs?*

This is a difficult modality to evaluate, as changes occur on both system and individual resident levels and there is no guarantee in the short run that a system change (such as reduction of fragmentation between the informal and formal helping systems) will also result in a measurable positive change among elderly community residents. In fact, evaluation measures need to be targeted to those specifically involved in the intervention as well as to the older persons in the community at large.

OBSTACLES AND LIMITATIONS

There are a number of obstacles, some of which have been mentioned above, that may make it difficult to implement this intervention modality. High levels of administrative support are required for an intervention that may be threatening to staff and particular elements in the community. Highly specialized skills are needed to conduct the intervention. Furthermore, because of the potential for conflict, it may be difficult to secure necessary funding.

There are also several limitations. Community empowerment is a process modality that may show results only in the long term. Thus agencies will be asked to devote significant staff resources for a somewhat controversial strategy that may show no short-term benefits. Not all agencies may be willing to do this, and many agencies will not receive the support of their boards or funding sources. Furthermore, because of the need for specialized skills, this strategy probably is not feasible in all agencies or in all communities. In some communities older residents may be burdened with issues of survival (i.e., food, clothing, and shelter) that preclude the successful implementation of long-term power strategies.

CAUTIONS

This model has some tendency to produce negative or hostile reactions by community leadership if the activity is perceived as being used to make an attack on them. Therefore, the worker must help the community members to determine what strategies will be most useful in order to decide when a "consensus model" is more appropriate than a "conflict model" (Cox et al., 1979). Staff must also help community members to determine when the conflict model is preferred, and if the battle can be won, since there is little help given to people when they are set up for failure. Staff must avoid conflict for its own sake and avoid confusing means and ends.

Another caution is that issues the worker identifies as critical may not be the issues most appealing to the older persons in that community.

Sometimes their issues are more pragmatic, short term, and crisis oriented. It is important, therefore, for staff to be carefully restrained, so that they do not offer strategies and tactics that are unsuitable to the older persons involved. Staff must also let the process govern and must abide by the community's right to decide.

A final caution is that this modality needs to focus on long-term process, not merely on short-term products. Thus the development of a self-help group may be a product outcome of the empowerment modality, but, more important , it is also a means in the process — namely, building power and strength for the community.

EXERCISES AND STUDY QUESTIONS

1. Your agency serves a working-class community containing many elderly persons. There are a number of ethnic, fraternal, and social organizations to which the elderly belong. There is also a large number of churches in the community and the clergy are very active in community affairs. How would you utilize the community empowerment intervention to enhance the power of the elderly in the community? What would you do and why? Which groups or organizations would you involve? What obstacles might you face? How can these obstacles be overcome?

2. Is the community empowerment intervention an appropriate one for your agency? Why? Why not?

3. How would you address the resistance and/or hostility to the use of community empowerment by staff, community groups, agencies, or funding bodies?

4. How would you determine when to use community empowerment rather than other intervention modalities such as case management or neighborhood helping?

SUGGESTED READINGS

Cox, F., Erlich, J., Rothman, J., & Tropman, J. (Eds.) (1979). *Strategies of community organization*. Itasca, IL: F. E. Peacock.

Crossman, L., London, C., & Barry, C. (1981). Older women caring for disabled spouses: A model for supportive services. *The Gerontologist, 21* , 465-470.

Naparstek, A., Biegel, D., & Spiro, H. (1982). *Neighborhood networks for humane mental health care.* New York: Plenum.

CONCLUSION

This volume has attempted to aid practitioners in understanding what social networks are and the roles they play with older persons in order to emphasize how human service agencies can intervene to strengthen existing support systems and to create new ones when needed. As can be seen by the various program examples and the discussions of professional roles and implementation issues, such work can be innovative, exciting, and fruitful. It can also be difficult, because it may involve the development of new skills and behaviors and perhaps a different way of looking at human needs and resources. Also, as we have indicated throughout this volume, there are dangers, obstacles, and limitations to social network interventions. We recapitulate below the most salient of those issues.

ISSUES IN NETWORK INTERVENTIONS

Social network interventions represent a new way of looking at the delivery of human services to those in need. Most agency workers are used to a professional model of service delivery in which the worker is usually the direct deliverer of services. Although family and friends of the client are sometimes called on for assistance, the worker's role often is still the central one. As we have seen in this volume, however, there are a number of social network intervention modalities in which workers' roles, though important, are not supreme. In these interventions workers often are in partnership with the informal support system and work as linkers, enablers, catalysts, organizers, or supporters rather than as direct providers of services.

Social network interventions should build on the strenghts and resources, not weaknesses, of clients and their social networks. All too often professional human services workers and agencies concentrate primarily on the problems of clients and do not pay sufficient attention to areas of positive functioning and strengths. Network interventions emphasize maximizing the capacities of individuals, families, and communities.

Social network interventions focus on *communities* as well as *individuals*. In addition to the development of services based on meeting the needs of individual clients who have asked for services, agencies must examine unmet needs on a community basis and assist existing groups and organizations in that community to respond to those needs. Professional roles involve working through and with other resource providers to develop programs and services and to highlight the vital and central roles of older persons in the community.

Social network interventions require *flexibility*. Agencies should not try to fit the community's needs into the agency's structure and framework, but rather to respond to how the community itself defines its problems and needs. To illustrate, several years ago a college in New England opened up a new campus and put down sod, instead of sidewalks, between all the buildings. After one year, the college dug up the areas where the sod had been most worn away from walking and put sidewalks in these places. Analogously, for social network interventions to be most effective, agencies need to learn how individuals, families, and communities naturally solve problems and meet needs in order for agencies to graft professional interventions onto these natural processes.

Agencies must recognize the need for "flexibility" in social network interventions. There must be flexiblity in the use of funds to enable demonstrations of innovative projects such as those used in the State of Maine, where family members are paid to deliver services to relatives in an attempt to lessen institutionalization of the frail elderly. Staff time also must be used flexibly and creatively. Some interventions require considerable preparatory or development time before any programs actually begin. If the process is unnecessarily shortened in the short run to save dollars, in the long run the interventions probably will not be maintained successfully. Staff time may be needed before or after traditional working hours, such as during evenings or on weekends. The staff will be called to assume new and perhaps different roles. Staff must show flexibility in assuming these roles, and they must receive the necessary training, supervision, consultation, and administrative supports.

The agency administrator must be supportive of the need for social network interventions and provide necessary training and supervision for staff who are developing these new thrusts. Without this strong support, these interventions cannot succeed. Administrators have to encourage staff in these attempts and seek to secure flexibility to use monies in different ways than in the past. If the regulations of existing funding bodies do not allow this, then administrators need to seek special funding for demonstration projects. New and different yardsticks have to be developed to measure the work of staff and to reward time and efforts in the area of network interventions.

Many social network interventions seem to require either a central facility or coordinating body that serves as a resource for coordination, supervision, continued support, and referral when the informal sector discovers a problem more appropriately handled by a formal service. The need for a central facility appears to be especially salient to certain types of programs, such as service exchange programs and social support groups.

DANGERS, OBSTACLES, AND LIMITATIONS OF NETWORK INTERVENTIONS

Social networks can do harm as well as good. Some networks may be judgmental or require conformity. Other networks may be ineffective in dealing with difficult individuals. Networks can enforce notions of pride and privacy, leading individuals to avoid seeking professional help when such care is warranted.

Several years ago, the President's Commission on Mental Health issued its final report on the nation's mental health needs. Its first recommendation called for recognition, understanding, and utilization of informal support systems to address the mental health needs of the nation's population. The commission cautioned that informal support systems should not be seen as a rationale to cut needed professional services. Despite this caveat, the worst fears of many of those involved in social network interventions have come true. Needed professional services are indeed being cut, and families, friends, neighbors, and other informal service providers are being asked to pick up the burden. There is a very real danger that such action can seriously overload and weaken informal support systems.

Another danger is that professionals might not fully understand the difficulty and time required to develop social network interventions. They may attempt "cookbook" replications of successful projects, without regard to the process involved or the skills and training needed by staff. Such interventions may have the unintended effect of weakening rather than strenghtening informal support systems. Finally, there is the danger of romanticizing informal support systems and failing to realize that such systems are not always positive, can sometimes do harm as well as good, and may not be suitable to deal with all problems and issues.

There are also a number of obstacles that may prevent full utilization of social network interventions. Professionals may not be knowledgeable about the role and functions of informal support systems or may believe that only those with professional education and training should offer help to people in need. Informal helpers, in turn, may be intimidated by professionals and may be uncomfortable interacting with them. Professionals may not have the necessary skills for assessing and intervening with informal support systems. Depending on the intervention, specialized skills may be needed in counseling and therapy, consultation, group work, or community organization. Although not all staff need all these skills, a particular intervention may require additional training and expertise by agency staff. This may be especially burdensome because of current cutbacks of public and private dollars for training. This suggests another obstacle: Some interventions may take a considerable amount of staff time in the beginning to develop, and the agency wishing to undertake the intervention may not have the funds or the time with which to do so. In fact, as the public dollar becomes tighter, many agencies are being forced to deliver only treatment or clinical services. Social network interventions of a preventive nature, like many of those we have discussed, many not be supported.

Other obstacles include administrative, fiscal, and legal procedures of funding bodies and service agencies that may mitigate against social network interventions. Most aging network agencies are reimbursed on a unit of service basis for agreed-on services. If we expect these agencies to utilize informal networks, then reimbursement formulas must reflect this new role.

Finally, in terms of limitations, the current state of evaluation of social network interventions needs to be examined. As we have seen, although most network interventions have endeavored to undertake at least some type of evaluation, these evaluations are somewhat primitive. Some projects have not been evaluated at all; others have been evaluated either through client self-reports or through anecdotal program reports. Only a few interventions have utilized before-and-after measures, and if so, rarely with a control or comparison group. There is need for more thorough and scientific program evaluations not merely to ascertain the relative success of the intervention but specifically to assess which components seem to be successful for which participants and whether particular intervention strategies are more successful than others. Agencies can often obtain assistance from local colleges, universities, or health and welfare councils in undertaking such evaluation. A key question in future evaluations is the relation between professional and informal services: Are some needs met more appropriately by professionals and others by the informal network? What is the proper balance of informal and professional services? How can we maximize the most efficient use of both types of support systems?

CONCLUSION

This volume has attempted to describe, analyze, and prescribe approaches for the utilization of social support systems for older persons. The work is new and exciting; the challenge is great. The efforts of workers and agencies to build on and add to our existing knowledge base will enhance the quality of life for all older persons and their supportive others.

REFERENCES

A stronger project. GOH serves the Fairfax elderly. (1982). *The Cleveland Foundation Annual Report 1981.* Cleveland, OH.

Acccounts: Newsletter of Generational Interaction for Today. (1982). *26* (Spring), *27* (Fall).

American Foundation for the Blind. (N.D.) *What are friends for? Self Help groups for older persons with sensory loss.* New York: The U.S.E. Program.

Antonucci, T., & Bornstein, J. (1978). *Changes in informal support networks.* Research Report, NIMH Grant #MH-14618.

Baer, B., & Federico, R. (1978). *Educating the baccalaureate social worker: Report of the undergraduate social work development project.* Cambridge, MA: Ballinger.

Barnes, J. A. (1954). Class and committees in a Norwegian island parish. *Human Relations.* *7* (1), 39-58.

Barnes, J. A. (1972). *Social networks.* Reading, MA: Addison-Wesley.

Baum, M., & Baum, R. (1980). *Growing old: A societal perspective.* Englewood Cliffs, NJ: Prentice-Hall.

Biegel, D. (in press). The application of network theory and research to the field of aging In W. J. Sauer & R. T. Coward (Eds.), *Social support networks and the care of the elderly: Theory, research, practice and policy.* New York: Springer.

Biegel, D., & Baum, M. (1983). *Social networks and the frail elderly interview schedule.* Pittsburgh: University of Pittsburgh School of Social Work.

Biegel, D. & Naparstek, A. (Eds.). (1982). *Community support systems and mental health: Practice, policy and research.* New York: Springer.

Biegel, D. & E., & Naparstek, A. (1982). The neighborhood and family services project: An empowerment model linking clergy, agency professionals and community residents. In A. M. Jeger & R. S. Slotnik (Eds.), *Community mental health and behavioral-ecology.* New York: Plenum.

Biegel, D. E., & Sherman, W. R. (1979). Neighborhood capacity building and the ethnic aged. In D. Gelfand & A. Kutzik (Eds.), *Ethnicity and aging.* New York: Springer.

Bott, E. (1957). *Family and social network.* London: Tavistock.

Brice, G. C., & Nowak, C. A. (1982). *Education as a family mental health intervention.* Presented at the 35th Annual Scientific Meeting of the Gerontological Society of America, Boston, MA.

Brody, E. M. (1982). Older people, their families and social welfare. In *The Social Welfare Forum, 1981.* New York: Columbia University Press.

Brody, E. M. (1977). Cited in C. A. Nowak & G. C. Brice, *A review of familial support systems in later life: Implications for mental health and social service providers.* Unpublished paper, Center for the Study of Aging, State University of New York at Buffalo.

Butler, R. N. (1981). Overview on aging: Some biomedical, social and behavioral perspectives. In S. B. Kiesler, J. N. Morgan & V. C. Oppenheimer (Eds.), *Aging: Social change.* New York: Academic Press.

Cantor, M. H. (1972). Life space and the support system of the inner city elderly of New York. *The Gerontologist. 15* (1), 23-27.

Cantor, M. H. (1979). The informal support system of New York's inner city elderly. In D. Gelfand & A. Kutzik (Eds.), *Ethnicity and aging.* New York: Springer.

Caplan, G. (1974). *Support systems and community mental health.* New York: Behavioral Publications.

Caplan, G., & Kililiea, M. (1976). *Support systems and mutual help.* New York: Grune & Stratton.

Cassel, J. (1976). The contribution of the social environment to host resistance. *American Journal of Epidemiology,* 102, 107-123.

Cohen, C. I., & Sokolovsky, J. (1981). Social networks and the elderly: Clinical techniques. *International Journal of Family Therapy, 3(4),* 281-294.

Collins, A., & Pancoast, D. (1976). *Natural helping networks.* Washington, DC: National Association of Social Workers.

Colman, V., Sommers, T., & Leonard, F. (1982). *Till death do us part: Caregiving wives of severly disabled husbands.* Gray Paper No. 7. Issues for Action, Older Women's League.

Cox, F., Erlich, J., Rothman, J., & Tropman, J. (Eds.). (1979). *Strategies of community organization.* Itasca, IL: F.E. Peacock.

Craven, P., & Wellman, B. (1973). The network city. *Social Inquiry, 43* (344), 57-88.

Crawford, L., Smith, P., & Taylor, L. (1978). *It makes good sense, a handbook for working with natural helpers.* Technical report, Portland State University School of Social Work.

Crossman, L., London, C., & Barry, C. (1981). Older women caring for disabled spouses: A model for supportive services. *The Gerontologist, 21* 465-470.

Crowe, A. H., Ferguson, E., Kantrowitz, B., & Biddle, E. (1981). *The elder program: An education model in network building among the elderly.* Paper presented at the 34th Annual Meeting of the Gerontological Society, Toronto, Canada.

Curtis, R. W. (1979). *The future use of social networks in mental health.* Boston: Social Matrix Research.

Dean, A., & Lin, N. (1977). The stress-buffering role of social support: Problems and prospects for systematic investigation. *Journal of Nervous and Mental Disease. 165* (6), 403-417.

Dlugokinski, E., Olson, R., Moran, D., & Rest, S. (1982) *Health care: Meeting the crisis through wellness networks.* Unpublished paper, G.I.F.T., Oklahoma City, OK.

Eaton, W. (1978). Life event, social supports and psychiatric symptoms: A reanalysis of the New Haven data. *Journal of Health and Social Behavior, 19,* 230-234.

Elderly Outreach Program. (N.D.) *The elderly outreach program.* Albuquerque. NM.

Ellor, J. W., Anderson-Ray, S. M., & Tobin, S. S. (n.d.). The role of the church in services to the elderly. *Interdisciplinary Topics in Gerontology, 17,* 9-131.

Fischer, C. S., Jackson, R. M., Stueve, C. A., Gerson, D., Jones, L. M., & Baldassare, M. (1977). *Networks and places: Social relations in the urban setting.* New York: Free Press.

Froland, C., Pancoast, D., & Chapman, N. J. (1979). *Professional partnerships with informal helpers: Emerging forms.* Paper presented at the annual meeting of the American Psychological Association, New York.

Garrison, J. E., & Howe, J. (1976). Community intervention with the elderly: A social networks approach. *Journal of the American Geriatrics Society, 24,* 329-333.

REFERENCES

Gelfand, D., & Gelfand, J. (1982). Senior centers and support networks. In D. Biegel & A. Naparstek (Eds.), *Community support systems and mental health: Practice, policy and research.* New York: Springer.

Germain, C. B., & Gitterman, A. (1980): *The life model of social work practice.* New York: Columbia University Press.

Getzel. G. S. (1981). Social work with family caregivers to the aged: A long-term care approach. *Social Casework, 62* (4).

Gordon, E. (1981). *Living with an elderly parent: The effects on the family, a literature review.* Jerusalem Research Department, The Ministry of Labour and Social Affairs.

Gore, S. (1978). The effects of social support in moderating the health consequences of unemployment. *Journal of Health and Social Behavior, 19,* 157-165.

Granovetter, M. (1973). The strength of weak ties. *American Journal of Sociology, 78* 1360-1380.

Gurland, B. et al. (1978). Personal time dependency in the elderly of New York City: Findings from the U.S.-U.K. cross-national geriatric community study. In *Dependency in the elderly of NYC.* New York: Community Council of Greater New York.

Guttmann, D., Kolm, R., Mostwin, D., Kestenbaum, S., Harrington, D., Mullaney, J., Adams, K., Suziedelis, G., & Vargo, L. (1979). *Informal and formal support systems and their effects on the lives of elderly in selected ethnic groups.* Technical Report. Final Report, AOA Grant #90-A-1007. The Catholic University of America.

Guttmann, D. (1982). Neighborhood as a support system for Euro-American elderly. In D. Biegel & A. Naparstek, (Eds.), *Community support systems and mental health: Practice, policy and research.* New York: Springer.

Gwyther, L. (1982). Caring for caregivers: A statewide family support program mobilizes mutual help. *Center Reports on Advances in Research. 6* (4).

Haber, D. (1983). Promoting mutual help groups among older persons. *The Gerontologist,* 23 (3), 251-253.

Haugk, K. (1976). The unique contributions of churches and clergy to community mental health. *Community Mental Health Journal, 12* (1), 20-28.

Hendricks, J., & Hendricks, C. D. (1977). *Aging in a mass society.* Cambridge, MA: Winthrop.

Herron, C. (1983, June 28). Grandmother waits for school bell. *Pittsburgh Post-Gazette.*

Hooyman, N. (1983). Social support networks in services to the elderly. In J. K. Whittaker & J. Garbarino (Eds.), *Social support networks: Informal helping in the human services.* Hawthorne, NY: Aldine.

Kahn, R. L., & Antonucci, T. C. (1981). Convoys of social support: A life course approach. In S. B. Kiesler, J. N. Morgan, & V. C. Oppenheimer (Eds.), *Aging: Social change.* New York: Academic Press.

Kulka, R. A., & Tamir, L. (1978). *Patterns of help-seeking and formal support.* Research Report, NIMH Grant #MH-14618.

Kuhn, M. E. (1978). Learning by living. *International Journal of Aging and Human Development, 8* 359-365.

Lauffer, A., & Gorodezky, S. (1977). *Volunteers.* Beverly Hills, CA: Sage.

Lawton, M. P., & Byerts, T. (1973). *Community planning for the elderly.* Washington, DC: U.S. Department of Housing and Urban Development.

Lieberman, M. A., & Gourash, N. (1979). Effects of change groups on the elderly. In M. A. Lieberman et al. (Eds.), *Self-help groups for coping with crisis.* San Francisco: Jossey-Bass.

Litwak, E. (1979). *Support networks and the disabled: The transition from the community to institutional setting.* Paper presented at the meeting of the Gerontological Society, Washington. DC.

Lopata, H. Z. (1973). *Widowhood in an American city,* Cambridge, MA: Schenkman.

Lowenthal, M. F., & Haven, C. (1968). Interaction and adaptation: Intimacy as a critical variable. In B. Neugarten (Ed.), *Middle age and aging.* Chicago: University of Chicago Press.

Louisiana Center for the Public Interest. (1982). *1982 Annual Report.* New Orleans, LA.

Maguire, L. (1983). *Understanding social networks.* Beverly Hills, CA: Sage.

Maguire, L., & Biegel, D. (1982). The use of networks in social welfare. In *Social welfare forum, 1981.* New York: Columbia University Press.

Mechanic, D. (Ed.). (1982). *Symptoms, illness behavior and help-seeking.* New York: Prodist.

Mechanic, D. (1978). *Medical sociology.* New York: Free Press.

Mellor, M. J. (1982). *Group services for caregivers of the aged: Who needs help?* 109th Annual Forum, National Conference on Social Welfare, Boston, MA.

Mellor, M. J., Rzetelny, H., & Hudis, I. (1981). Self-help groups for caregivers of the aged. In *Strengthening informal supports for the aging: Theory, practice and policy implications.* New York: The Natural Supports Program, Community Service Society of New York.

Mental Health Services of Southern Oklahoma. (1982). *Trained listeners corps training manual.* Ardmore, OK.

Mitchell, J. C. (Ed.). (1969). *Social networks in urban situations.* Manchester, England: University of Manchester Press.

Naparstek, A., Biegel, D., & Spiro, H. (1982). *Neighborhood networks for humane mental health care.* New York: Plenum.

Natural Supports Program. The Community Service Society of New York. (1981). *Strengthening informal supports for the aging: Theory, practice and policy implications.* New York: Community Service Society.

New York State Office for the Aging. (1982). *Practical help caring for an eldely person in the community: An informal caregiver's curriculum.*

Noberini, M. R., & Berman, R. U. (1983). Barter to beat inflation: Developing a neighborhood network for swapping services on behalf of the aged. *The Gerontologist, 23,* 467-478.

Nowak, C. A., & Brice, G. C. (1983). *A review of familial support systems in later life: Implications for mental health and social service providers.* Unpublished paper, Center for the Study of Aging, State University of New York at Buffalo.

Office of Aging Studies. (1979). *Training to enhance informal support systems of the elderly.* Final report to DHEW from the School of Social Welfare, Louisiana State University.

Palmore, E. (1974). *Normal aging II.* Durham, N.C.: Duke University Press.

Pancoast, D. L., & Chapman, N. J. (1982). Roles for informal helpers in the delivery of human services. In D. Biegel & A. Naparstek (Eds.), *Community support systems and mental health: Practice, policy and research.* New York: Springer.

Personal correspondence. (1983, June 17). With Voni Moore, Planner, Philadelphia Corporation for Aging.

President's Commission on Mental Health. (1978). *Report of the task panel on community support systems.* Washington, DC: Government Printing Office.

Riessman, F. (1965). The "helper therapy" principle. *Social Work, 10*(2), 27-32.

Rose, A. M., & Peterson, W. A. (Eds.). (1965). *Older people and their social world.* Philadelphia: F. A. Davis.

Rosow, I. (1967). *Social integration of the aged.* New York: Free Press.

Ruffini, J. L., & Todd, H. F. (1979). A network model for leadership development among the elderly. *The Gerontologist, 19*(2).

Ruffini, J. L., & Todd, H. F. (1981). Passing it on: The senior block information service of San Francisco. In M. P. Lawton & S. L. Hoover (Eds.), *Community housing choices for older Americans.* New York: Springer.

Rzetelny, H., Kasch, E., Toperman, E., & Hudis, I. (1980). *Supporting the caregiving efforts of family, friends and neighbors of the elderly: A community based multi-model approach.* Paper presented at the 57th Annual Meeting of the American Orthopsychiatric Association, Toronto.

Rzeteiny, H., & Mellor, J. (1981). *Support groups for caregivers of the aged: A training manual for facilitators.* New York: The Natural Supports Program, Community Service Society of New York.

Shanas, E. (1979). The family as a social support system in old age. *The Gerontologist, 9*(2), 169-174.

Shanas, E. et al. (1968). *Old people in three industrial societies.* New York: Atherton.

Shore, B. (1983). *Some salient aspects of aging as a guide to practice.* Paper presented at the Conference on Aging and Loss, National Association of Social Workers, Pittsburgh, PA.

Shore, B. K., & Raiff, N. (1977). *A conceptual model for relating informal and formal helping of systems.* Paper presented at the Council on Social Work Education, Annual Program Meeting, Boston, MA.

Shore, B., Yamatani, H., & Gordon, E. (1982). *Final report: Senior citizen service exchange.* Pittsburgh: University of Pittsburgh School of Social Work.

Silverman, A. G., Brahce, C. I., & Zelinski, C. (1981). *As parents grow older: A manual for program replication.* Ann Arbor: University of Michigan.

Silverman, P. R. (1970). The widow as a caregiver in a program of preventive intervention with other widows. *Mental Hygiene, 54,* 540-547.

Silverman, P. R. (1980). *Mutual help groups.* Beverly Hills, CA: Sage.

Slater, P. (1970). *The pursuit of loneliness: American culture at the breaking point.* Boston: Beacon.

Smith, S. A. (1975). *Natural systems and the elderly: An unrecognized resource.* Unpublished monograph, Portland, OR.

Smyer, M. A. (1982). Supporting the supporters: Working with families of impaired elderly. *Journal of Community Psychology.*

Snyder, J. (1971). The use of gatekeepers in crisis management. *Bulletin of Suicidology, 8.*

Spiegel, D. (1982). Self-help and mutual support groups: A synthesis of the recent literature. In D. Biegel & A. Naparstek (Eds.), *Community support systems and mental health: Practice, policy and research.* New York: Springer.

Spitler, B. J. C., Wachs, H. P., & Kobota, F. (N.D.) *Project Y.E.S.: A curriculum guide for high school youth serving the frail elderly.* Los Angeles: Institute for Policy and Program Development, Andrus Gerontology Center, University of Southern California.

Spitler, B. J. C., & Kobata, F. (N.D.) *Project Y.E.S.: A replication manual for high school youth serving the frail elderly.* Los Angeles: Institute for Policy and Program Development, Andrus Gerontology Center, University of Southern California.

State of Hawaii, Department of Social Services and Housing. (1982). *Case management procedures: Forms and instructions.*

State of Kentucky, Division of Aging Services. (1982). *Request for proposal for home care: Community based in-home services for the elderly.* Frankfort, KY.

State of Illinois, Department on Aging. (1982, September). *Community care.* Annual joint report to the Governor and the Illinois General Assembly on Public Act 81-202.

State of Maine, Department of Human Services. (1983, January 31). *Report on the home-based care program.* Unpublished report.

State of Rhode Island, Department of Elderly Affairs. (1982, December). *Family and community support systems: Final report.*

Suchman, E. A. (1967). *Evaluative research.* New York: Russell Sage.

Sussman, M. B. (1976). The family life of old people. In R. H. Binstock & E. Shanas (Eds.), *Handbook of aging and the social sciences.* New York: Van Nostrand.

Swenson, C. (1979). Social networks, mutual aid, and the life model of practice. In C. R. Germain (Ed.), *Social work practice: People and environment.* New York: Columbia University Press.

Teare, R. (1981). *Social work practice in a public welfare setting: An empirical analysis.* New York: Praeger.

Townsend, P. (1975). *The family life of old people.* London: Routledge & Kegan Paul.

Trimble, D. (1980). A guide to network therapies. *Connections: Bulletin of the INSNA. 3*(2), 9-21.

U.S. General Accounting Office. (1977). *Report to the Congress: The well-being of older people in Cleveland, Ohio.* Washington, DC: Government Printing Office.

Walker, K. N., McBride, A., & Vachon, M. L. S. (1977). Social support networks and the crisis of bereavement. *Social Science and Medicine, 11*(1), 35.

Wellman, B. (1981). Applying network analysis to the study of support. In B. Gottlieb (Ed.), *Social networks and social support.* Beverly Hills, CA: Sage.

Wolfe, A. (1978). The use of network thinking in anthropology. *Social Networks, 1,* 53-64.

Work Exchange, Inc. (1982). Unpublished program materials, Milwaukee, WI.

Worts, F., & Melton, K. (1982). *A guide to the utilization and support of informal resources to serve the aging.* Technical Report, North Philadelphia Initiative for Long Term Care. (Prepared for the Pennsylvania Department of Aging).

Zarit, J. M., & Zarit, S. H. (1982). *Measuring burden and support in families with Alzheimer's disease elders.* Paper presented at the 35th Annual Scientific Meeting of the Gerontological Society of America, Boston.

Zastrow, C. (1981). *The practice of social work.* Homewood, IL: Dorsey Press.

Zimmer, A. H. & Mellor, M. J. (1981). *Caregivers make the difference: Group services for those caring for older persons in the community.* Unpublished paper of the Natural Supports Program, Community Service Society of New York.

ABOUT THE AUTHORS

DAVID E. BIEGEL, Ph.D., is Assistant Professor, University of Pittsburgh School of Social Work. Prior to joining the University of Pittsburgh faculty in 1980, Dr. Biegel served as director of an NIMH-funded research and demonstration project that focused on strengthening social networks in urban ethnic neighborhoods. He is currently the co-principal investigator of a research and demonstration project that is examining social support networks of frail elderly individuals who are aged 75 and over. Dr. Biegel has written extensively concerning social networks, neighborhoods, and mental health. He is the co-author of two books about social networks, *Community Support Systems and Mental Health: Practice, Policy and Research* (New York: Springer, 1982, co-edited with A. J. Naparstek) and *Neighborhood Networks for Humane Mental Health Care* (New York: Plenum, 1982, co-authored with A. J. Naparstek and H. Spiro).

BARBARA K. SHORE is a Professor in the School of Social Work, University of Pittsburgh. She is a graduate of the Carnegie Institute of Technology and the University of Pittsburgh. Dr. Shore holds a bachelor's degree, a master's degree and a doctoral degree in social work, a master's of science in public hygiene from the Graduate School of Public Health. She was co-director of the university-wide Long-Term Care Gerontology Center for 3-1/2 years. Dr. Shore's recent publications include a chapter in the *Handbook of Social Services* (Praeger); an article being published this spring in the *Journal of Social Issues;* and a chapter in *Voluntarism and Social Work Practice, A Growing Collaboration,* edited by Florence S. Schwartz (University Press of America, 1984). Dr. Shore was principal investigator for an NIMH grant examining the social and psychological consequences of rape and has recently been principal investigator for two Pennsylvania Department of Aging contracts, and for a number of training grants from NIAAA and the NIMH.

ELIZABETH GORDON, M.S.W., is a doctoral student at the University of Pittsburgh School of Social Work. She is a social welfare researcher who has worked in a variety of settings in this country and abroad. She has been project manager of the Senior Citizens Service Exchange, a skills exchange network for the elderly, and project director of Strengthening the Social Networks of the Frail Elderly, a research and training project that culminated in a resource manual for service providers. Ms. Gordon is the author of a number of articles, among them "Analysis of the Impact of Labour Migration on the Lives of Women in Lesotho," *The Journal of Development Studies* (April 1981) and "Easing the Plight of Migrant Workers' Families in Lesotho," in W.R. Bohning, *Black Migration to South Africa* (The International Labour Office, 1981). Ms. Gordon's doctoral dissertation explores the relation between women's work careers and attitudes toward retirement.

WARNER MEMORIAL LIBRARY
EASTERN COLLEGE
ST. DAVIDS, PA. 19087